The Upstream Model

The Hidden Secrets

Hidden Secrets to Building a Massive Referral Business While Crushing Big Tech Competitors

JUSTIN STODDART

Copyright © 2020 by Justin Stoddart

All rights reserved. No part of this book may be used or reproduced in any manner whatsoever without prior written consent of the authors, except as provided by the United States of America copyright law.

Published by Best Seller Publishing®, Pasadena, CA
Best Seller Publishing® is a registered trademark
Printed in the United States of America.
ISBN: 9798585820977

This publication is designed to provide accurate and authoritative information with regard to the subject matter covered. It is sold with the understanding that the publisher is not engaged in rendering legal, accounting, or other professional advice. If legal advice or other expert assistance is required, the services of a competent professional should be sought. The opinions expressed by the authors in this book are not endorsed by Best Seller Publishing® and are the sole responsibility of the author rendering the opinion.

For more information, please write:
Best Seller Publishing®
253 N. San Gabriel Blvd, Unit B
Pasadena, CA 91107
or call 1 (626) 765 9750
Visit us online at: www.BestSellerPublishing.org

TO MY FAVORITE SEVEN PEOPLE ON THE PLANET

YOU ARE MY WHY

PRAISE FROM READERS OF *THE UPSTREAM MODEL:*

What Justin tactically walks us through in this book is a fail-proof way of insulating your business from disruption. Perhaps more now than ever before this is a message the business community has been missing and sorely needing. Regardless of industry, if all business is based on your ability to build and sell, then this one book will give you the foundation to build from. Although Justin is most known for getting his readers and listeners to think bigger, in this guidebook he breaks down how to build bigger while focusing on the simple!

> —**Chris Suarez, Principal Broker, PDX Property Group, Co-Founder & Co-CEO, Place Inc.**

The Upstream Model is a necessary read for any serious service industry professional to prepare for the coming wave of disruption from the world's tech giants and new lean startups. Differentiating and building trust are more essential to success in the service industries than ever before. Justin Stoddart's *The Upstream Model* is a practical guide on how to effectively and efficiently succeed in new client acquisition despite disruption and rising competition.

> —**Cory Mahaffey, Managing Partner, Northwestern Mutual Financial Network, Portland, Oregon**

It's not about the money, it's about BECOMING the best that you can be. I have discovered that 1's and 0's pay the bills, but the journey of "becoming" and the impact and influence created through one's pursuit of excellence is truly life changing. *The Upstream Model* will break down step by step what is necessary to become the leader required to influence and impact the lives of those you lead.

> —**Jeff Cohn, Owner, KW Elite, Elite Real Estate Systems, The Team Building Podcast**

A must read! Justin hits it out of the park with *The Upstream Model.* If you want to increase sales, increase customer acquisition, and increase retention ... this is what you need! A shift is taking place in sales. Unless adoption of new ways of aligning with customers is realized, businesses will be in jeopardy. Justin's Upstream Model clearly defines the path and should be adopted by anyone in sales. I've seen Justin use and showcase the concepts of this book to propel him to the top! Success leaves clues, and this book is full of them. Adjust to the new marketplace with this well-written gem. Thank you for this gift Justin!

—David Bravo, Jr., CEO, Monarch Title

Justin is not only a thought leader in the real estate industry, he is someone who provides tactical, real-world solutions to his audiences. He never stops delivering incredible value and is always in search of new answers to questions many people haven't yet considered. I highly recommend you read this book!

—Jim Remley, Real Trends Top 500 Broker, Speaker, Author, and CEO of eRealEstateCoach.com

Since the day I met Justin Stoddart, he established himself as a trusted partner, rather than a solicitor—someone looking to provide significant value before receiving anything in return. Soon, I was referring every client his way, and even began encouraging many others to do the same. *The Upstream Model* will become a catalyst for many businesses and sales professionals to not only survive but thrive in the face of growing automation and big tech competition!

—Trevor Hammond,, C.L.A., C.M.P.S., Branch Manager, Coach to Mortgage Professionals, Author of *Borrow Smart, Repay Smart* and *Mortgages, Money and Life*

Finally, a book that explains and clearly demonstrates the power of networking with a simple analogy. Justin's thoughts resonate with me, and I would echo what he said in the book: *"You'll find that you are much more empowered to influence and lead people by taking an interest in what is going on in their life than by trying to get them interested in you."* For 28 years I have built my business doing this very thing. This book is written as a guide to quickly teach you how to not just build relationships but change your behavior. This allows you to have both strong relationships and profit.

—Jay Marks Broker, Owner, Jay Marks Real Estate

Most salespeople spend their lives chasing clients and leads. If you're looking for a better way, *The Upstream Model* is your answer. Imagine having partners and allies that introduced you to new clients well before they started talking to your competition! That's exactly the kind of big thinking and planning you'll learn from Justin Stoddart, who has implemented this model in multiple businesses.

—Nick Krautter, Principal Broker, City & State Real Estate, Author of *The Golden Handoff*

Justin has created a simple, implementable approach to staying relevant in this new tech-driven world. Capturing the key relationships to move upstream will always move your service business in the right direction. Failure to succeed after reading this can only be due to the reader choosing not to do what Justin lays out in this book.

—**Tim Clairmont, CFP®, MSFS™, LACP™, Founder & CEO, Investment Advisor Representative, Clear Financial Partners®, Author of *Passionate Ambivalence* and *What Should I Do With My 401k?***

The only thing we can't get enough of is time. In a world that continues to move faster, we need to think and work strategically to protect both our time and income streams. Justin has given us a perfect model to do just that. Rather than talking to 100 people to get to 100 customers, why would you not talk to one person to get to 100 customers? Doing so gives you more income in less time. This is a must-read for anyone wanting to grow a relationship-based business to the highest levels.

—**Patrick Woods, Operating Principal of Keller Williams Realty, Elk Grove, Chico, and Roseville. Real Estate Team Owner, Leadership Coach**

This book is fire!!! I just finished it one sitting. We teach our agents similar concepts, but this book adds even more depth and thought to the process. If you build your network the right way, you won't have to cold call anymore. Instead, clients will be cold calling you! This book gives you a blueprint on how to do that. It's all about building systems while also building relationships. This book is so spot on.

—**Justin Bosak, Owner/Partner, RE/MAX Revolution, The Oceans Six Group, Host at *Finding Success Radio***

Justin Stoddart, host of the "Think Bigger Real Estate Show," brings to you the principles, strategies, and tactics that are critical for you to apply TODAY in your business! In his book, *The Upstream Model*, he outlines the steps to take now in order to disrupt the disruptors which have their sights set aggressively on your business, as well as the mindshare and loyalty of your customers! Justin clearly outlines the models and principles which are foundational in building a massive referral business while launching you ahead of your competitors in today's fiercely competitive service-based industries! A must-read!!

—**Laura Gillott, Gillott Home Team, #1 Team in Oregon per Real Trends and #100 in the nation**

Justin's model for growing your business with a reliable source of strategic referral sources is both timely and critical in today's quickly changing world. If you are a service-based professional, you know the value of consistent lead generation and the importance of your primary referral sources. With tech-enabled companies disrupting our business world, business owners and professionals should be focused on modeling the rise of Netflix versus the fall of Blockbuster. Justin not only outlines how to discover the upstream opportunities in your business but provides the roadmap to execute these strategies in your business today. As someone who has been following Justin's podcast, I am excited to put these tactics to work in my business to become an upstream professional!

—**Kevin Owens, Real Estate, America's Top 100 Agents, top 5% in the world**

This is a timely message from a unique messenger. In sales, thinking bigger often means imagining a bigger scale, but with *The Upstream Model*, we are urged to think bigger about the scope of when and how we can provide value to our prospective customers. We can no longer wait until that end user is ready to make that buying decision. That is becoming too late as disruptors improve their craft. But we can disrupt the disruptors by doubling down on our value, our humanity, and becoming more strategic. *The Upstream Model* is a simple and clear way to imagine doing your business in the future with more profit and ease.

—**James Adair, Mortgage Loan Officer, Sierra Pacific Mortgage**

You have to gain trust. In the age of big data, artificial intelligence, technology, and commoditization, sales professionals have to make sales differently from the past. To win in today's world, you will have to gain faith from others. If you want to succeed in business, I recommend that you read *The Upstream Model*. Justin Stoddart shows you the way in this book.

—**Dan Rochon, Broker, Head Coach, Owner, Virginia Sales Network,** Author of *Real Estate Evolution*

Knowing where to fish—and what tools to use—is the difference between an amateur and a professional. Justin's Upstream Model is brilliant, as it helps to equip us with all the skills necessary to catch that big whale! Insightful, clever, and easily digestible ... these three elements make for a fabulous formula!

—**Erik Hatch, Realtor, Owner, and Broker, Hatch Realty,** Author of *Play for the Person Next to You*

As a social entrepreneur, I have found that Justin's "Think Bigger Real Estate Show" has always delivered amazing content. *The Upstream Model* has followed suit. I own several companies in healthcare, real estate, title and mortgage industries, and I'm always sharing Justin's content with my salespeople and executives. *The Upstream Model*, put a different way, is stepping over dimes to pick up a dollar. Share this book with your sales team today. If not, you are losing money!

—**Joseph McCabe, CEO, Re/Max Affiliates, Home Front Mortgage**

What a wonderful read! *The Upstream Model* is a practical yet simple model to follow in business and life. I wish Justin's insight would have been available when I began my career in real estate, as it would have saved me years of following the shiny objects and, ultimately, frustration. This is a must-read for any business professional who is looking to grow a bigger business while deepening relationships. *The Upstream Model* will be required reading for everyone on my team.

—**Ben Andrews, Broker, Owner, Next Home Realty Group, Author of** *The Long Run*

Justin has always been the type of person to add what I perceive as "real value." Value comes in many different forms and the only way you can understand that is by becoming part of someone's business. You have to understand what someone really wants or needs to earn their business. That's what Justin does every day. He is a true practitioner of his craft and he lays out the perfect blueprint in *The Upstream Model*.

—**Jesse Dau, Broker, CEO, The YouTube Agents**

Instead of worrying that massive technology companies will take over your industry and put you out of work, I highly recommend that you read *The Upstream Model*. This book does a masterful job of sharing ideas and examples for growing your business and yourself. The book's solid ideas for developing strong relationships with your key referral partners is something that will allow you to not only survive but thrive in an increasingly competitive world. This is a great resource for all professionals who want to take their careers to new heights!

—**Patrick Galvin, Author of** *The Connector's Way*

Not only has Justin established himself as a leader in the podcast world with his "Think Bigger Real Estate Show," now he's brought to light something anyone in sales or any industry for that matter must stop and think about. The content of this book will radically change the way you go about business as well as view many aspects of life.

—**Marc Fox, Principal Broker, CEO, Fox Real Estate Groups**

Justin is like my iPhone; I don't do business without him. His insights and thoughts within *The Upstream Model* are an excellent way to grow a long-term profitable business. It's one of the many ways Justin encourages us to *go think bigger*.

—Heather Robbins, CEO, Principal Broker, Robbins Realty Group

For years, the biggest competition real estate professionals faced was each other. Oftentimes, to be more successful than the agent down the street, you simply had to maintain a consistent relationship with your clients. Now, competitors in the form of venture-backed Big Tech are flooding the real estate space. They're using shiny new technology to steal your clients and erase you from the transaction. In *The Upstream Model*, Justin lays out exactly how you can continue to beat your competition, old and new, using the tried and true tactics of relationship building, amplified by "going upstream." If you want to future-proof your business, making it untouchable by Big Tech, you need to read and implement the steps in this book.

—Cody Martens, Founder/CEO, Luminary Agent

It all starts with thinking differently. *The Upstream Model* turns traditional thinking on business relationships and creating new business on its head. This is a must-read for all entrepreneurs and business owners!

—Pat Mancuso-Entrepreneur, Coach, CEO Mancuso Consulting Group

We all know that a referral-based business is so much more fun and less stressful than buying and chasing leads. The question is, how do we find enough people who will refer business to us? The answer may surprise you. The answer is that you don't need as many referral partners as you may think. The answer is *The Upstream Model*. This book reveals a simple, yet powerful, strategy that you can begin using today to completely transform your business. I highly recommend this book to every agent who wants to build a sustainable, profitable business through referral partnerships.

—Amy Donaldson, Sales Performance & Leadership Coach, Author of *Get Off the Cash Flow Roller Coaster*

Justin has built an audience and a following through the "Think Bigger Real Estate Show" by providing massive value and opportunities to grow your business and your life. With *The Upstream Model* he's done it again. Referral and recommendation are the heart and the starting point to any real estate business. Justin's stories and recommendations help make this point incredibly clear and also put real estate professionals on a path to generate enormously successful businesses by helping them maximize their most valuable asset: their database.

—Gus Munoz Castro, Founder & CEO, Power ISA

We wholeheartedly support Justin's Upstream Model to combat industry disruptors. Our mantra is "People don't do business with a logo. They do business with a person." And partnerships are made between people, not technology. His concept of "improving your identity in the marketplace to that of mentor and leader" is spot on. Presenting yourself as valuable and unique is what separates the order-taker from the dream maker. On a personal level, Justin is one of the most genuine thought leaders in the industry, and when he presents a thought-provoking concept, we know its purpose is to serve as a rising tide that raises all ships.

—**Tonya Eberhardt & Michael Carr, Co-Owners of BrandFace, Co-Authors of *BrandFace for Entrepreneurs***

The Upstream Model lays the foundation for a very important conversation that every service-based business owner should be having. How do we outmaneuver the major tech giants that are out to replace our expertise in exchange for convenience? Justin not only raises some extremely important questions but he also lays out an easy to implement framework that solves them.

—**Eli Schmidt, Broker, Owner, Mile High Property Brothers**

If lead generation or marketing has baffled you, Justin's book, *The Upstream Model*, will unlock that mystery. His approach is authentic and experienced, as is his "Think Bigger Real Estate Show," which helps us all every day to focus on reducing the bottlenecks in our businesses. *The Upstream Model* is a must-read for all who want to do better!

—**Tamie Brown, Broker, Robbins Realty Group**

In the real estate game, there are far too many people spending way too much and getting very little results. Justin's brilliant *The Upstream Model* is one of the solutions to this very problem. His simple, yet compelling strategies will help you work smarter not harder. This is a must-read for anyone in the real estate industry.

—**Robby Trefethren, Real Estate Coach, Hatch Coaching**

Service professionals face new competition and increased pressure on their businesses and lives. Justin Stoddart shows a proven and timeless model to serve clients better, get more business, and have more fun doing it. *The Upstream Model* will be the model that local professionals use to win during the current and future tech wars.

—**Josh Friberg, Speaker, Trainer, Coach**

This book is well written and will give the reader access to think beyond ordinary. I also enjoyed reading the family stories and how they are connected to becoming successful. A must read!

—**Amir Fathizadeh, Coach, Author of *Gossip, The Road to Ruin***

CONTENTS

Preface: Disrupt the Disruptors 1

Chapter 1: The Dangers of Thinking Small 9

Chapter 2: Predicting & Preparing for the Future 23

Chapter 3: Cold Market, Warm Market & the Need for an
Alternative Market 37

Chapter 4: Discovering the Upstream Model 47

Chapter 5: The Upstream Model Applied to You 65

Chapter 6: From Vendor to Peer to Mentor and Leader 87

Chapter 7: Your DATA Base 103

Chapter 8: Extending Your Reach 115

Chapter 9: The Charge to Lead 125

Chapter 10: Time for Bigger Thinking 137

PREFACE: DISRUPT THE DISRUPTORS

Your future as a well-paid professional within a service-based industry is in serious jeopardy. Whether it be real estate, mortgage, insurance, wealth management, or similar, it is time to pay attention to what is happening. Little by little, your customers are warming up to the easy, safe, convenient and non-committal benefits of your complete or partial replacement by ever-advancing technology offerings.

Whether you recognize it or not, you are competing against multi-million- and multibillion-dollar companies—the tech disruptors in the form of wholesalers, lead aggregators, digital portals, online marketplaces, and the like. Well-known examples include Zillow, Redfin, Quicken Loans, Geico, Progressive, Vanguard, and E-Trade.

Although you may argue that these disruptors can never take your job entirely, they have already taken away some of your profit margin and even some of your customers, and it won't stop there. In other industries, tech giants like Amazon and Google continue to connect consumers directly to products and services once offered by profitable businesses and lucrative professions. Experts predict it's just a matter of time before these and other behemoths move more aggressively into service-based industries like yours.

In this battle waged for the attention and loyalty of your prospective clients, you cannot outspend these competitors, nor will you defeat them at their game. Your hope for victory—a profitable business and a bright, autonomous, and prosperous future—lies in superior business models that allow you to harness and leverage the power of technology while magnifying your competitive advantages. These include being human, having relationships, and impacting people in very individual and personal ways. An unwillingness or inability to grow and adapt accordingly will lead to one of the following undesirable outcomes:

1. You own an unprofitable business that pays you subsistence wages to work around the clock while you wear out your health and your relationships.

2. You become a lower-paid functionary/sales and service representative of one of these disruptive technology companies.

3. You are forced out of your industry altogether.

While one of these scenarios will befall many, it does not have to be *your* fate; with help, your future can look very different. Where there is disruption, there is always opportunity. Some would even argue that the bigger the disruption, the bigger the opportunity.

In the chapters that follow, there is an evergreen roadmap called the Upstream Model, which will help to make a sustainable future a reality. More importantly, you will be doing all of this in a way that keeps you from also sacrificing everything else in life that matters even more, like your health and relationships.

THE INCEPTION OF THE UPSTREAM MODEL

In my mid-20s, I was newly married and working for a general contracting company that specialized in building luxury custom homes. I still remember the day my dad flew into town to visit me, my wife, and our baby girl. My dad has always been one of my biggest supporters: he coached my sports teams when I was little, drove to the far ends of our state to watch my high school football games, and, to this day, finishes most of our conversations telling me what a privilege it is for him to be my dad. He's a special man and I love making him proud.

On this particular visit, I was excited to take him on a tour of one of the million-dollar homes I was building at the time. Very few moments have compared to his reaction when he stepped foot inside. The look on his face and the enthusiasm in his voice told me he was pleased with the businessman and provider I was becoming.

However, on that day I kept something hidden from my dad. What he could not see, and what we did not discuss, was that behind the scenes of those big, beautiful homes lurked uncertainty and anxicty that came from a question continuously running through my mind: *Where is my next deal going to come from?*

As eager as I was to make him proud, I was just as eager to not let him down. Throughout my childhood, I watched my dad, who came from very humble beginnings, work tirelessly and sacrifice dearly to start and grow businesses. Some of these ventures were very successful while others were a total bust. Throughout all the ups and downs, his motive was to provide a good life for our family.

While he thought that a good life for us meant a comfortable home and a boat for our vacations, the good life he actually provided for us was two things that were far more valuable: he gave us an example of what it takes to succeed and he gave us a better starting place than his own to create our own success stories. Considering how hard my dad worked, both of these gifts were an inheritance I dared not waste.

It was under this added accountability to do well that an important realization emerged. I now know that this fact, if not quickly learned and embraced, becomes the primary reason why most businesses fail:

Every business must always be engaged in two fundamental activities, in this order,

ATTRACTING CLIENTS > SERVING CLIENTS

Regardless of how good you are at serving clients, every business owner must never forget that its first and foremost responsibility is to attract new clients.

Although I regularly felt fired up and excited about the many possibilities unfolding before me, including that of eventually branching off to start my own general contracting company, this harsh reality was staring me down. My company, my family, and my coworkers and their families were counting on me to be successful at attracting clients—not just once, but over and over again. Without enough clients to serve, my knowledge, systems, and processes for building million-dollar homes were all irrelevant to me, to them, and to everyone.

As a business owner you have likely felt this same pressure. The persistent question we all face is *From where will my next deal be coming?*

As I set out to solve this problem for myself, I uncovered a model that also answers this question for others. Additionally, the model provides so much more, including the following:

1. A consistent new stream of referrals to qualified clients who see you as an expert.

2. Higher commissions and margins.

3. Less time commitment needed to attract new clients.

4. Improving your identity in the marketplace to that of mentor and leader, helping you to rise above the threats of industry disruption.

UPSTREAM MODEL PREVIEW

The following image gives you an idea of how the Upstream Model works:

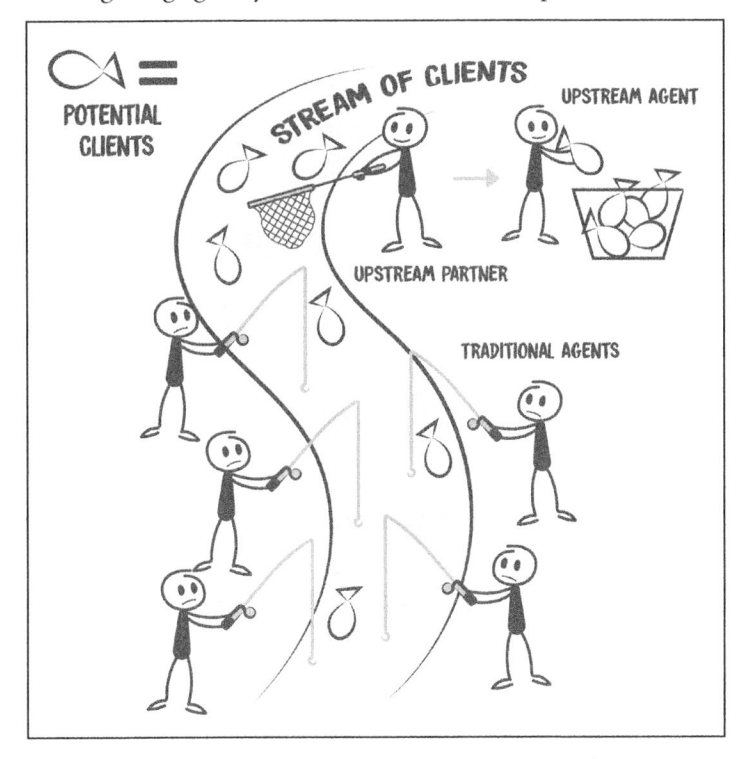

The Upstream Model teaches you how to get more referrals from fewer relationships while teaching you not just how to do, but how to become. As you rise above the thinking, practices, and value propositions of a *traditional professional* and become an *upstream professional*, you'll be moving out of the reach of industry disruption.

While many of our examples will be from and about real estate agents, know that the principles, strategies, and tactics are applicable across all well-paid professional industries.

In the chapters to come, you will learn the following:

- Why learning and applying this model is important and urgent.

- How to identify upstream partners from other industries who are having regular conversations with your potential future clients.

- Why these upstream partners are not currently referring that business to anyone in your industry.

- How to position you, your brand, and your value proposition in such a way that your upstream partners want to bring you into the conversations with *their* clients willingly and repeatedly. They will do it not just because they know you, like you, and trust you. They will do it because they need you.

Most importantly, the model will teach you how to think bigger. It will teach you that there is a relationship-based approach that allows you to reach the highest levels of production and profitability while maintaining a tremendous quality of life.

MY STORY

My mission and my passion are to help you to think bigger—to recognize the potential within you and then to inspire and help you to live in pursuit of that potential so that you can live, give, and serve abundantly.

For the past 20 years, I've had the good fortune of building businesses. While I did enjoy many components of being a homebuilder, I grew to understand that my interests and strengths are more about developing people not land, and about building businesses not homes. Consequently, I've been able to build a brand, a business, and a career in which *working in* my business involves helping others to *work on* their business. I do that through my business development role within the real estate industry, as the host of a nationally syndicated podcast, the "Think Bigger Real Estate Show," and as leader of the Think Bigger movement.

My combined mission, passion, and experience now bring me to you as a guide, helping you to understand and rise above the threats we all face by understanding and implementing the Upstream Model. Throughout this book I am going to be directing you to where I have added additional resources, essential for helping you to get the maximum value from the model, harnessing its full potential as a critical blueprint for your profitable future in this endlessly disruptive era. You can find these important resources at *upstreammodel.com*.

I'm excited for you. Even amidst—especially amidst—industry disruption, your future is very bright so long as you continuously learn to **GO THINK BIGGER!**

1
THE DANGERS OF THINKING SMALL

The head football coach continued giving me a tour of my new school and, pointing into another room, he smiled enthusiastically. Eagerly awaiting my reaction, he said, "This is the computer lab, and those computers are all connected to the internet."

That was the first time I remember hearing the word "internet." I smiled politely, pretending to know why that was a big deal. I was confident that this coach could never compare to the coach I was leaving behind at my previous school.

As a naturally positive and happy person, I wanted to be excited to be there. Yet, things both above and below the surface made this time of my life especially challenging. I was a junior in high school, and my family and I had just moved to this new town, leaving behind my dreams of playing out my senior football season with my closest friends.

One month prior, in December 1995, my former teammates and I had just won our second state football championship in only three years. During this time, our win-loss record was 37 wins and only one loss.

Considering the starting core of our team was returning underclassmen, high school sports experts expected us to win it all again. Ever since the eighth grade, we dreamed and talked of winning the state championship our senior season. Considering the success that we had already had, this seemed to be an inevitable reality. That was until, as a family, we made the decision to move two hours north to a suburb of Portland, Oregon, called Wilsonville. The motive for our move was to get both of my parents closer to their business's biggest customers while extending a lifeline to their struggling marriage.

While it was uncommon for the head football coach to be the one offering a new student a tour of the school, this situation was different. Hoping to reduce the impact of the move, my amazing mother had reached out to create a special bond with this head coach and his wife. To Coach, I was the catalyst he was looking for to get his football program out of startup mode and the slump of their previous winless season. As a result, he had taken particular interest in me.

As we walked into the computer lab, I reflected on my previous school in a small rural town. There, we had just one computer in each classroom and then one additional room in the school dedicated to typewriters and word processors for keyboarding class. Instead of computers, resources in Junction City went toward more "practical" purposes, like the woodshop, metalworking building, and an automotive repair shop—all very fitting for the skills and interests of that small town and its residents.

"Yes," Coach continued. "Every computer you see is connected to the worldwide web," he said, trying again to impress upon me just how advanced my new school was. He then brought me over to one of the computers, clicked on a little icon labeled "Netscape," and we waited while the peculiar page loaded.

To me, this technology was not particularly remarkable at the time. I had no concept and no vision of how this "internet" thing would change the world. I didn't realize that those who learned to harness its power would have seemingly endless opportunities. To me, it seemed unnecessary. The school and environment that I was coming from had things figured out. After all, we were the undefeated state champions.

DOING WHAT YOU'VE ALWAYS DONE

As a junior in high school, I was thinking really small, blind to the fact that the internet would change our world in countless ways. As a professional, I've learned that similar naïveté concerning technological advancements can be professionally lethal, which is especially true when your industry sits in the crosshairs of Wall Street and venture-backed technology disruptors.

If you're thinking to yourself, "What I'm doing is working, and I don't see the need to change," I ask you to consider my variation of an old adage: *If you do what you've always done, you will **NOT** get what you've always gotten. Instead, you will get less and less and less.*

That "NOT" is not a typo. Doing what you've always done will only get you what you've always gotten *only if all other variables also stay the same*. You and I both know that all other variables in our industries and our world are not static; we live in a very dynamic and rapidly changing world. Take, for example, how quickly the world changed as result of COVID-19. Within just a few days, all major sporting and entertainment events were canceled, and many businesses closed. Most other companies had to adapt to figure out how to serve their customers differently, including enabling much of their workforce to work from home.

To do as one has always done looks a lot like the Apple, Samsung, and Blackberry stories. Two adapted to change and customer usages, one did not. What phone are you looking at right now? The lesson here is simple: Don't be the Blackberry.

Successful businesses and professionals are all about adaption, forward thinking, and preparation. Thinking what you've always thought, doing what you've always done, and continuing to be who you've always been will undoubtedly get you *less* in the form of

- fewer transactions,

- eroding margins through lower commissions and higher customer acquisition costs, and

- diminished professional identity and brand, which means that fewer people will see you as being valuable enough to be at the center of their transaction.

Now is the time to double down on learning and implementing strategies that will offer dividends for your future business growth and success; I know because I've had to do it time and time again.

DRIVERS OF DISRUPTION

As we settle into accepting that what we have always done will not get us what we have always gotten, we open ourselves up to predicting the future and our happy, autonomous, productive, and profitable place in that future. But what do you know about the threat of industry disruption and its impacts?

Knowledge advancement impact: In 1982, architect, inventor, futurist, and author R. Buckminster Fuller released a book called *Critical Path* in which he shared his findings of the increasingly rapid rate at which human knowledge was expanding. Congruent to these findings, he made some predictions that he called the Knowledge Doubling Curve.

For example, beginning at 1 AD, human knowledge was estimated to take approximately 1500 years to double. By 1900, it was taking only every 100 years for the knowledge that we had to increase that much. Then, just forty-five years later, in 1945, the time in which human knowledge was doubling had dropped to every twenty-five years. By 1982, when Fuller's book was released, human knowledge was doubling at the staggering rate of every twelve to thirteen months!

It doesn't stop there. All of this had happened before the widespread PC era and, of course, the internet. In 2013, the computer information technology giant IBM, who brought us Watson, one of the first glimpses of the power of artificial intelligence (AI), predicted that by 2020 (yes, you read that right), human knowledge would be doubling every *twelve hours*!

Although hard to fathom, the rise of AI and machine learning is, once again, *changing everything*. This predicted and rapid technological advancement, coupled with the mindset and skillset of upcoming generations, is no doubt driving disruption.

Generational impact: The Millennial generation grew up with the internet. The generation that follows them, Gen Z (or Centennials), grew up with social media. While Millennials are increasing in their purchasing power and influence, the oldest Centennials are already graduating from college and starting to enter the workforce. The impact of these generations fully embracing these technologies is causing all of us to be more reliant on tech and less reliant on human-to-human interactions than ever before.

Case in point, how many Amazon deliveries will arrive at your house this week? If your home is anything like mine, it is more than one. In our microwave society, not only have we as consumers become accustomed to shopping online, now waiting for anything that takes longer than two days has become a severe inconvenience. Naturally, we now compare every customer experience we have with what Amazon and others have done to lower cost and complexity while increasing comfort and convenience.

Consumer demand impact: When industry leaders build protective moats around their professions through legislation rather than through embracing innovation, a void between an industry-standard and the experience that consumers want begins to develop. Much of this demand for a better experience stems from the client experience to be found in other industries.

Going back to our Amazon example, I have yet to meet anyone who doesn't love their Prime membership, which delivers almost anything in two days or less. However, when our clients bring that same expectation for fast service into our industries and we're unable to deliver, whether reasonable or not, clients get restless. When consumers get restless, investor-backed visionaries begin working to fill that white space.

One example of a technology disruptor working to fill the white space of a sometimes slow and complicated mortgage process is Rocket Mortgage with its catchphrase "Push Button, Get Mortgage." Whether or not choosing your largest liability on your largest asset from an app on your phone with little to no consultation is good for the client is another question. Nevertheless, that innovation is resonating with millions as it fills the consumer need of decreasing complexity and increasing convenience.

Another example is found by asking almost anyone who is actively shopping for real estate what is their preferred home search tool. Both you and I would put money on the fact that their answer will be the apps and search tools offered up by disruptive technology companies like Zillow, Redfin, or Realtor.com, instead of services offered by the local real estate multiple listing service.

Quality impact: Not all real estate agents and professionals from other similar service-based industries take their business as seriously as you do. In fact, with low barriers to entry for getting started in many industries, less committed and less professional agents representing your industry are not uncommon. Consider the repercussions every time a consumer feels like their expert of choice didn't represent them as a true fiduciary and didn't offer the professionalism and value consistent with the fees that the industry historically demands. The likelihood of that client and their immediate circle being more susceptible to a tech-friendly alternative on their next transaction undoubtedly increases. This lack of professionalism can show up in many ways, including

- the means, methods, and manner in which agents go about getting new clients,
- a lack of care for and communication with their clients during the transaction, and
- a general lack of knowledge and experience that inhibits the agent from being able to serve their clients at a high level.

Opportunity impact: Let's look at the residential real estate market as an example. In the United States alone, this market was worth $33.6 trillion as of January 2020. For easy math, let's just assume that 6 percent in commissions get paid out on that asset to real estate agents once every 10 years as that property changes hands. That equates to over $200 billion in commissions up for grabs each year. The slice of that commission pie is a big enough opportunity that disruptors and their investors are willing to invest heavily in the following ways:

- Building a technology supplement or technology alternative to a traditional professional

- Educating the consumer on a new way of doing business

- Discounting the fee to the consumer

- Having an attractive enough return for the tech investors

While the long-term return to investors is still unproven for many of these disruptors, there is no question that the objective of these groups is to minimize what you do and get paid while offering a tech solution that they can monetize at scale.

Innovation impact: Any time there is an economic downturn, businesses have to cut costs to survive. Cutting payroll is often the fastest way to realign their expenses with their lower revenues. As automation steps in to fill that void, those jobs often never return, even after the economy recovers. Once it has been built, opportunists begin looking for ways to apply that technology in other sectors.

We saw this during the Great Recession that started in 2008, and we see it happening again as a result of the COVID-19 global pandemic.

FOLLOW THE MONEY

In case you needed additional convincing that industry disruption is real, ongoing, and will somehow affect you eventually, here are a couple of points to consider. First, we can't ignore the money trail in real estate and other industries. As reported in *Inman News*, according to GCA Advisors (an investment bank that tracks various types of funding), in 2018 alone there were 289 investment deals done in real estate technology totaling $5.4 billion. This total was an increase of 84 percent year over year for the past several years. Specifically, in September 2018 *alone*, $2.7 billion was invested in real estate tech. (Putting that in perspective, less than $500 million was invested in all of 2013.) Zak Schwarzman, a partner at

MetaProp, a New York City–based early-stage venture capital firm called that $2.7 billion investment a "jaw-dropping amount of capital by any measure."

So why, you might ask, is real estate technology becoming such a popular space for investors to put their money? The oversimplistic answer is that those who invested those billions are seeking a return and are bullish that they'll get one.

While there is a massive amount of money flowing into these disruptors, not just in real estate but in many service-based industries, not all of it goes toward developing the technology. A healthy percentage goes toward marketing and advertising with a focus on changing the consumer mindset about *you*, the service professional. Their goal is to encourage consumers to start to ask some of the following questions:

> "Will an agent/mortgage loan officer/insurance agent/financial advisor give me something I cannot get online?"

> "Is there a cheaper/faster way to do it and still get the same result?"

The objective of these tech companies is to answer those questions with these two overarching answers:

> "The level of service that the consumer will get from a technology-based offering will be equal to or even better than that of a traditional agent."

> "The only difference is that we can do it for less money (and often quicker) than a traditional agent."

SHOULD I BE CONCERNED?

I suspect that, like their professional friends from other industries, busy residential real estate agents are responding to this question with a monologue that goes something like this:

> *Justin, I'm just going to do a good job for my clients, and I'm sure it will all work out. I really don't have the bandwidth to worry about being "disrupted." My list this week includes: finding my next lead,*

showing homes, making and receiving offers, reviewing multiple offers, inspections, negotiations, addendums, in escrow, back out of escrow, in escrow again, preliminary title reports, broker demands, docs, paperwork, signings, following up with the lender, title companies, contractors, appraisers, all while hoping and praying for closings. That doesn't even take into account the things I should have on my list! Like staying in contact with my sphere, updating my CRM, following up on those open-house leads and the potential clients who told me to call them back in a few months, and planning out the details of my upcoming client event. Not to mention being present daily on social media.…

And one more thing. I also have, or would like to have someday, a life outside real estate that involves my kids' soccer practices, their homework, family dinner, chores, friends, date night, the gym, personal growth, and some other forms of me-time. Isn't that the real challenge I should be worried about, Justin? How do I get all of that done?

Besides, if industry disruption is out of my control, wouldn't it be wise to not worry about it?

While your list is legit and your final argument is valid, I would invite you to consider the following. While the most productive people in the world focus only on those things within their control, the most *successful* people in the world also anticipate the changes and position themselves to take advantage of it. The often-over-quoted advice from Wayne Gretzky applies here: *"A good hockey player plays where the puck is. A great hockey player plays where the puck is going to be."*

What Should Concern You

Consider this. You have excellent clients that love you. Yes, the ones who gave you great reviews after your last transaction and have also referred you to others. These are the same clients who thanked you profusely for the gift you offered at closing and then even showed up at your recent client event that you put on. Yes, even the very best clients are confronted regularly and subtly with the question as to if they should use you, a full-service professional, on their next transaction.

"Not my clients! We just agreed that they love me," you proclaim.

To which I would reply, I'm sure they do, but this isn't about how they feel about you. It is about where your clients' attention goes whenever they have a curiosity about your industry; they often go to the tech disruptors. It's about the constant inundation of marketing messages that follow from these same sources, not to mention that convenient little button on the technology disruptor's heavily trafficked website that invites sellers to get an immediate offer on their home. These messages are planting the seed that maybe, just maybe, there is some better, more modern way to do business. The subtle (some might even say mischievous) message offers up the idea that you can get a similar result while paying less on your next transaction by using a different, more technology-based model.

For financial advisors, it can show up in the form of those pesky little solicitations from your big tech competitors offering investment advice and vehicles that show up on Mint.com, that all-too intuitive online budgeting tool. While Mint.com is free to the consumer, they monetize through these advertisers that seek to poach your clients and the investments they have with your firm.

Like me, you've probably fielded questions about the value of a full-service professional in an industry that is not your own. For example, if you're a real estate agent, I'm sure you've had conversations with clients about whether they should use a mortgage loan officer or go with a mostly technology offering like the Quicken Loans Rocket Mortgage. Or maybe you've heard the debates about a local State Farm agent versus Geico. Know that when you are not around, consumers are asking the same questions about the validity and value of your value offering as well.

So, in short, should you be concerned about industry disruption?

Yes, and that concern should lead you to be vigilant and innovative in your practice to ensure that your relationships, your value proposition, and your positioning in the marketplace allow you to rise above these threats.

Will the Upstream Model help you to do this?

I'm glad you asked. Yes, it will.

TIME TO MOVE ON

It was almost 20 years later that I took a trip down memory lane. With my wife and young family in tow, we rolled into Junction City, past the junction of Highways 99 East and West that had given the town its name. It felt as if very little had changed in this small town. As Interstate 5 took the place of Highway 99 as the primary highway running north and south in our state, I couldn't help but make the comparison between what I was seeing and the bygone town of Radiator Springs in the Disney-Pixar movie *Cars*.

As we drove further into town, I started to bust out the glory stories. You know, the ones where dad is a total hero. I recalled the vivid memories of being on a charter bus late at night with my fellow teammates as we returned to town from winning another state championship. As if it were yesterday, I remembered the full police escort accompanying us after midnight from the edge of town, down the streets where community members had come out of their homes to cheer for us. Meanwhile, friends and family waited for us in our school parking lot under the big tiger mural, freshly painted on the outside wall of the gymnasium. There, they greeted us with hugs and high fives as we emerged from our bus like complete celebrities.

For just a moment, my kids looked at me differently. With a look of awe on their faces, it was if they were having a hard time picturing a time when I, their dad, was once athletic and cool. Then, like a balloon that loses its helium, my heroic story began to deflate as we pulled into that same parking lot. "Your school looks really old, Dad." I was just glad they didn't add, "Kind of old like you, Dad."

I, too, was surprised at what I saw. The school building looked like there had been no updates in those 20 years. Sitting just adjacent to the old metal shop, and across from the automotive repair building, sat our football practice field. Rather than being well-groomed as it had remained in my mind's eye, I saw weeds and unkempt grass. As I looked to my right, I noticed that same large tiger mural was now sun-faded and cracked. I later learned that the football program that once went nearly undefeated for three straight years had now failed to win even one game in its most recent season. The school that, in my mind, had it all figured out had been left behind.

In contrast, my new high school in Wilsonville had a different story to tell. Not only did my new head coach become one of the most influential men in my life but under his inspired and innovative leadership, Wilsonville also won a football state championship of their own. The school has now become known and admired for its academic and athletic accomplishments.

You've surely noted the parallel between my two schools and the choice we have to make concerning our careers. Regardless of our "championship accolades" of days past, things are changing quickly. If we don't think bigger than we have in the past by innovating and moving to where things are going, we will be left behind. We can think small, choose to disregard the signs of change, continue doing what we've always done, and assume we'll get what we've always gotten. Or we can accept the fact that disruption is real and will have an impact on not only our margins but also potentially our businesses and careers altogether. As media influencer and icon Gary Vaynerchuk teaches, our choice is simple. We can choose to "innovate or die."

In our next chapter, I am going to share with you two things that will shore up the foundation upon which you will build your understanding of the Upstream Model. Explicitly, these two things will teach you how to see disruption coming as well as give you an understanding of how to navigate above and beyond it.

ASSERTIONS

- *Doing what you've always done will not get you what you've always gotten. In a rapidly changing world, it will get you less and less and less.*

- *Recognize and accept that technology is going to continue to improve at faster and faster rates and that it will continue to do things that you once did.*

- *Recognize and accept that many well-paid professionals are going to be replaced or severely minimized by technology.*

- *Recognize and accept that not all professionals will suffer this fate and that you don't have to be among those who do.*

- *Recognize and accept that to survive and thrive, you will have to become even more valuable than you are now to the clients you serve.*

REFLECTIONS

Reflect honestly on whether you have been reluctant to innovate and change because of what you have accomplished in the past.

———————————————————————————

Do you see any risk in that? If so, why?

———————————————————————————

Have you chosen to use a technology disruptor over a professional in another industry, not your own (insurance, wealth management, CPA, etc.)? If so, why?

———————————————————————————

What can you learn from that and apply in your own business?

———————————————————————————

2

PREDICTING & PREPARING FOR THE FUTURE

I drive by a little building in my town that once was occupied by a psychic-reading business. It was just a few years ago that law enforcement uncovered this location as the setting of a very sophisticated "Sweetheart Swindle Story." As reported on ABC's *20/20*, a "fortune teller" (more like "fortune stealer") conned a wealthy timber heir out of $15 million of his family's money in just a few years.

The "psychic" posed as someone who was a friend, a confidant, and someone who was going to guide the wealthy heir to the life he'd always dreamed of. The psychic brought in her own family members as a cast of impostors to help her to patiently pull of the massive and subtle heist from the trusting heir.

As the vulnerable man continued to live a simple life, his con artist "psychic" and her real family lived a lavish life. They racked up a bill of over $600,000 at Nordstrom alone, millions of dollars in travel, a million-dollar home, and other properties. As if that wasn't enough, they also purchased multiple sports cars worth a quarter of a million dollars or more each.

While you cannot relate to the gullibility of the conned timber heir, you can definitely relate to the desire to continuously improve your life. Though I would never recommend putting your trust in "psychic powers," know that there are prudent predictors of the future that can act as a guide to moving you toward that better life. These predictors, when coupled with a model that is based on timeless principles and that magnifies your competitive advantages, can help guide you toward this desired, improved life.

PATTERNS AND PRINCIPLES

The first way we can more accurately predict the future while building our understanding and implementation of the Upstream Model is to observe other industries that have already been more severely impacted by disruption. To make this as applicable to our respective businesses as possible, we must train our minds to look for both patterns and principles. To illustrate how to do this, I'll highlight just two industries.

Retail. As a kid, the anticipation and experience of back-to-school shopping at the mall created some lasting memories for me. My mom would load up us three kids, drive to the mall, and haul us from store to store amidst crazy traffic and crowds. We each had an allotment of funds we could use in any way we wanted, dispensed with an occasional snippet of parental wisdom like, "If you buy those shoes, you'll have no money left for pants."

My brother, who has always been a bit cooler than me, would use his money for one or two articles of designer clothing from some hip store and then work paper routes to fill out the rest of his cool-kid wardrobe. Meanwhile, JCPenney and I did just fine together, and with my non-designer jeans and some white t-shirts, I was good to go. Looking back, it's no wonder he was more popular in high school, though I'm sure the fact that he's taller, darker, and more handsome than me didn't hurt either.

Fast forward 30 years to today. Have you been through a mall recently? It's kind of sad to see these large, often ostentatious buildings looking a little lonely, if not vacant. Sure, around the holidays, they still seem to have a bit of the hustle and bustle that is fun for some and infuriating for others. But what about the rest of the year?

Although the mall provided an experience that some found enjoyable, what was imperceptible at the time was how less expensive and less complicated online shopping would one day become.

Do you think either my wife or I take our kids to the mall for back-to-school or Christmas shopping now? Only out of total necessity. If we can buy it online, we will. Rather than loading up the car with a brood of small kids to haul them to, and chase them through, the mall, playing a seemingly endless game of hide-and-go-seek under clothes racks with our joy-filled and curious toddlers, my wife goes on Amazon. She shops dozens of providers, reads reviews, clicks, and—boom—packages are delivered within two days, sometimes even faster. Not to mention this all happens without any shipping costs other than our annual Amazon Prime membership.

Yes, there is a great convenience in that. But what if something goes wrong? "Oh wait, you don't like what showed up? No problem—just print out a return label and send it back! Oh, and by the way, you'll do this without ever leaving the comfort of your own home."

At least in my wife's opinion, the conveniences and lack of complexity far outweigh the costs of having to ship something back.

What did Amazon do? What is the pattern that they and other innovators and disruptors followed that we too must learn? They reduced the price, which included the costs of hauling kids to the mall, and they simplified the proposition by allowing you to shop the world's largest marketplace with features like reviews, "Buy now with 1-Click," and "Amazon Prime with Free Shipping," and then these packages arrive wherever you choose. All of this accomplished with the convenience of your mobile device.

Before I move on, I want to ask you this question, which points to an important principle:

Is there ever a time when the traditional model of retail makes more sense than just buying it online?

You'll have to answer that question for yourself. For me, certain things are either expensive enough or complicated enough that I don't feel comfortable making a purchase without expert counsel. I bring this up because embedded in the lessons of disruption within the retail industry is another vital takeaway, a principle if you will, that will help us predict the future and forge our way forward.

The risk of buying shoes you don't like and having to send them back is a little inconvenient, but it doesn't have significant implications on your life, your net worth, or your realm of future possibilities. Whereas, with real estate, with wealth management, with tax advice, and with insurance, making a misinformed decision can often have significant implications. Any industry that has the potential, through one transaction, to move a client's wealth needle from positive to negative must be looked at and treated differently than those that don't. Real estate, for example, needs to be looked at differently than retail, and we have the responsibility to educate our respective marketplaces of this principle.

Travel: In the real estate industry, we often hear, *"I fear that real estate agents will become the travel agents of the future."*

The rise of websites like Expedia and Travelocity have rendered travel agents all but extinct. Within the confines of trips that require only "functionary duties," like booking a flight from here to there or booking a hotel and rental car, that would be a fair assessment since online portals are less expensive and less complicated than the traditional model. The pattern is that service-based industries are all moving in that direction.

Just like I'm not going to go to the mall while hauling little kids to pay more for something that I could buy for less with just a few clicks on my phone, I'm also not going to visit a travel agent to book a simple flight from Portland to Los Angeles. It's just not necessary. However, consider what we might learn from another example.

I once sat in a meeting of a large and successful real estate team in Portland, Oregon, and heard the following story from an insurance agent and referral partner who was also in attendance:

> *My wife and I are planning a trip to Europe. Realizing the number of tools and resources that the internet provides, I went to work studying where to visit, eat, stay, and so forth.*
>
> *This experience caused me to quickly become completely overwhelmed by the number of reviews and information available. A lack of information was not a problem. The problem was the abundance of information. I couldn't possibly know what to trust or how to process all of it.*
>
> *In the end, I decided to hire a travel agent. I needed someone who had done this for others before to help me interpret the information, customize it for me, meet my wife's wishes and requests, and make decisions that would meet our goals for the trip.*

Isn't that interesting? Being the trip of a lifetime, the risk of getting it wrong had profound implications. Even though he could have booked it all online, with access to plenty of reviews and suggestions, he chose to pay to have someone guide him through the process. Because there were so many opinions and so many options, and because the risk of not getting it right was so high, he needed to have someone interpret the data to help him make decisions based on what his specific goals entailed.

With so much data and so much information available, your industry's customers often need a guide to interpret and help them to apply this information to themselves and their unique current situation and future goals. Creating algorithms to take the place of excellent advice on real estate, financial, legal, tax, or business consultation is difficult. But the big tech players in the service industry have done a great job omitting from their message the value that a well-incentivized expert advisor brings to the relationship.

But the reality still is that if you get bad real estate advice, tax advice, legal advice, wealth management advice, or insurance advice, you can't just print a label and mail it back. You can't just catch another flight to fix the problem. This advice and these offers have a much more significant impact on someone's net worth; therefore, having a trusted professional who can advise you becomes more and more critical.

You have likely identified several patterns and principles from the couple of examples above. Here are a few to get you started, which prime your mind to look for more moving forward:

- Businesses and professionals that thrive are those able to lower costs and reduce complexity.

- For the clients, the higher their risk of getting it wrong themselves, the more they are willing to pay professionals.

- Every transaction in which a client can do just as well or better using an all or mostly technology-based offering will eventually unload the added cost of a well-paid professional.

- Not all buying experiences are easy to replace with an all or mostly technology-based replacement.

- Your profession impacts people's net worth in significant ways, making you valuable and necessary.

- Value is defined as the difference between what you as a professional give versus what you charge. The greater your value, the more likely you are to be invited to remain at the center of the transaction.

As we look deeper at the disruption and innovation happening in other industries, our minds will become better trained at identifying the useful patterns and principles that emerge. This practice builds a more solid foundation on which we will apply our understanding of the Upstream Model. This then moves our respective value propositions, our margins, our businesses, and ourselves, beyond the reach of industry disruption.

RISK VERSUS REWARD RATIO

The backdrop to all of this that we must not ignore is that we live in a convenience-seeking world, sometimes called the "Now Economy." That name stems from our desire for, and the internet offering, immediate access to endless streams of information and options at any given time.

As if takeout food isn't convenient enough, we now have Uber Eats. As if Amazon Prime, delivered in two days, isn't fast enough, we now have Amazon Now, which moves the delivery window up to two hours. You get the picture. We want what we want, and we want it now, and technology has done a fantastic job of offering us some incredible conveniences. Facetiously, one might even say that we are all a bit like Veruca Salt in the classic story *Charlie and the Chocolate Factory*, who proclaims, "I want it NOW, Daddy!"

Amidst this "Now Economy," convenience is abundant. However, logic forces us to ask the counter question: *Is there a downside to all of this urgency and all of this convenience?*

If we don't make a few key distinctions, then yes, there can be a downside. Consistent with and similar to the patterns and principles we identified from the retail and travel industries, the downside is that being in a rush could cause us to miss the fact that there are specific buying and selling decisions that have a more significant impact on our net worth, and the net worth of our clients and prospective clients, than other decisions. Around these decisions, we should pause to consider how we must navigate as consumers and how you, as a well-paid professional, must step up and into the lives of your clients and prospective clients to best lead them in these decisions. Therefore, a critical factor in your ability to help your clients and prospective clients includes being able to help consumers understand the risk/reward ratio of competing choices.

This term, the "risk/reward ratio," is used to help investors to minimize risk and maximize return. It illustrates the prospective risk or reward an investor can earn on every dollar invested. Let's look at an example. An investment with a risk/reward ratio of 1:7 suggests that an investor is willing to risk $1 for the prospect of earning $7. Alternatively, a risk/reward ratio of 1:3 signals that an investor should expect to invest $1 for the possibility of making $3 on his investment. Obviously, the 1:7 ratio is a better situation for the investor.

Now, consider that as real estate clients and prospective clients go about making buying and selling decisions, first the real estate agent and then the client need to have an awareness about the subtle and not-so subtle indoctrination coming from deep-pocketed big tech. These messages convey that clients (or the investor in the risk/ratio example above) can increase their reward (the money they receive at closing) by using a lower cost tech option for their transaction. Technology disruptors preach that by using their online, discounted service, the client will get the same service as if they use you as their professional. In other words, the risk of using the tech offering is 1. On the other hand, the reward, meaning the money they get at closing due to reduced agent fees goes up. Small risk and a big reward—that sounds like a good deal for the client, right?

If this narrative is not interrupted and challenged, the client would naturally see this as a compelling offer against using a well-paid professional. The way to interrupt this narrative is to help the client to see that the risk of using a mostly tech offering is not 1. The value that you bring to your clients compared to the value that a mostly tech offer provides is not the same. In this example, in which your prospective clients are deciding whether to use a well-paid professional or a discounted mostly tech option, your strength comes in being able to demonstrate and communicate that the potential risks of not using you are higher than your clients have been led to believe.

Raising the risk (the first number in the ratio from 1 to something greater) can be done by illustrating the cost to the clients if something goes wrong or not as well as it could have gone, or if there is a missed opportunity altogether. As the first number in the ratio, the risk, goes up in the mind of the client, then the overall ratio drops and the reward (any savings or benefit that they may have been collecting from choosing a mostly tech offering) becomes less exciting. For example, if the risk/reward ratio was 2:3, the reward (the second number) is overshadowed by the increased risk.

When intentionally pursued and communicated, bringing the risk/reward ratio to zero, or even inverted to a negative number, is not difficult for a smart and skilled agent. A negative on the risk/reward ratio would entail that it costs the client money to **NOT** have you a part of their transaction. Being able to substantiate and communicate this point puts you out of reach of tech disruptors.

Here's an example of the risk/reward ratio in action. A mostly tech real estate brokerage, powered by low margins and high volume, fails to correctly price, stage, market, represent, or negotiate a transaction and it costs a client $10,000 on a $400,000 sale price.

That same broker offers a fee that was 2 percent lower than your fee to get the business. The risk was $10,000 and the reward was $8,000. In other words, this client/investor risked $10,000 to retain, $8,000 in discounted fees. That equates to an inverted risk/reward ratio, which would be a bad idea for investors.

For you math nerds, the risk/reward ratio inverts to 5:4. In other words, there is 1.25 times more risk to the client than there is a reward. Obviously, this would not be a wise investment decision for the client.

Rarely, if ever, is it the right decision to take a substantial risk for a small reward. Your clients, your prospective clients, and your upstream partners, which will be more clearly introduced shortly, all need to understand this—even if just at a conceptual level. They need to understand that the risks of not having your expertise working for them in their transaction far outweigh any reward of paying less to a tech offering.

Not only do they need your expertise in the transaction, they also need you to educate them to better understand the downside of doing business without having you as an expert in their corner. It also becomes critical for you to begin thinking in these terms and documenting specific stories from a myriad of different customer types and customer scenarios in which this expertise and value are apparent.

IDENTIFYING AND COMMUNICATING RETURN ON INVESTMENT

More than ever before, we in our respective well-paid, service-based industries must recognize and accept that traditional providers are no longer entitled to the client. We must find additional ways to boost our respective value propositions so that our clients and prospective clients see themselves as being best served by having us well-paid and at the center of the transaction.

Here are some additional tactical ways to think and communicate this value.

Identifying Return on Investment (ROI). Similar to the risk/reward ratio, you must begin to consider the fees that you charge not just as payment for services rendered. Instead, you and your clients need to see those fees as an investment that earns the client a positive return.

Think about that for a minute. If you had an investment in which you put in $1 and got out $1.50, or $2, or more, would you hesitate at all to invest in that $1? The obvious answer is, "I would not hesitate at all!"

With technology increasing both the quantity and the quality of lower-priced options around us, your chance as a professional for remaining at the center of the transaction becomes secure as you can provide, document, and communicate this positive return.

You may be thinking right now: "Justin, it is not always possible to demonstrate a positive ROI on the fees that I charge." My rebuttal is that if the only identifiable and documentable value you bring to the table is within the parameters of the transaction, then you will continue to struggle with this. The amount of value that you bring to a client must extend well beyond the parameters of the sale. I would even argue that the benefit of using you should also extend beyond the confines of your profession and industry.

What if you were to make regular and intentional introductions, recommendations, and referrals to your clients that allowed them to either

- grow their businesses;

- get a promotion within their respective job; and/or

- obtain tax, legal, or business advice that saves them tens or even hundreds of thousands of dollars?

In so doing, your fee just produced a positive ROI.

With the examples mentioned above in mind, I strongly encourage you to consider ways in which you are already adding significant value to your clients, as well as additional ways you could add value.

Additionally, I then invite you to begin to make this part of your ongoing value offering and client presentation. The more that you start to standardize and even systematize the regular addition and communication of this elevated level of value, the more your value will dwarf that of disruptive technology.

Communicating ROI. I want to emphasize the importance of communicating this value. It is not enough to have our value far outweigh our fees if the client doesn't see it or understand it.

You remember the philosophical question: *If a tree falls in the forest but there is no one around to hear it, does it make a sound?* In this analogy, the sound that comes from a tree falling is your value. If you don't communicate your unique value, much of it will go unnoticed, and then there will be a question as to if it exists at all.

In very natural ways, you must be helping your clients to understand what is happening in the transaction and the value that your expertise brings to the table.

Great professionals have the habits, systems, and processes to reach out to a client at systematic and predetermined times during the transaction to communicate in a natural, human, and genuine way to let the client know two things: what just happened in the client's transaction and what's coming next.

Although a few professionals deliver this beneficial information, it's not going to be enough moving forward. Technology firms can quickly write algorithms that do a good job of delivering information, and they already have. You need, therefore, to go beyond the practice of keeping your clients informed. Reiterating as often as makes sense the conversations that highlight the return that your unique and highly valuable expertise brings will take your value in the eyes of your client to a new level. Here are some suggestions:

1. Here's what just happened in your transaction: Now, the common or typical thing to do here would have been to do "X." Instead, we did "Y" because I wanted to better position you to avoid these threats [specify] and to take advantage of these opportunities [specify], which equate to this value [specify] to you.

2. Here's what's coming next: In this situation, a common thing to do here is to [specify action]. Instead, to avoid the threat or risk of [specify outcome] and to take advantage of the following opportunities [specify], I would recommend we take these steps instead. By doing this, we will see the following benefit of [specify] to you.

While doing this every time you communicate with your clients is surely overkill, implementing this pattern in natural and genuine ways will do several different things for you:

- Cause you to think in terms of creating uncommon levels of value

- Create accountability to serve your clients at a level that your competition doesn't even know exists

- Make a clear distinction between you and the typical professional, even between you and what technology algorithms can offer

- Create a clear difference in the minds of your clients and prospective clients of the value that you bring

In so doing, you're not just setting yourself apart from other professionals, you are also demonstrating that your value far outweighs your fees, which is an even higher level of communication. You're showing that although there *are* other options and providers, *you* are the only option that can lead to the best possible outcome.

Additionally, your fees are no longer shoppable to tech disruptors or others because the value that you bring is so much higher than what the alternatives are offering. You've systematically illustrated and communicated this value to clients.

BACK TO THE FUTURE

Maybe, like me, you once dreamed of how nice it would be to have the experience that the character Biff from the movie *Back to the Future II* had in getting a visit from his future-self, carrying a sports almanac that gave him a perfect roadmap to incredible fortunes. Or, maybe you've wanted to, like the conned timber heir, tap into psychic powers to know the best way forward to get the life that you want.

While I wouldn't advise holding your breath that a sports almanac or your local psychic shop are going to offer the guidance you're looking for, I am confident that what we have learned thus far, and what you're about to learn, will be very valuable to you in predicting the future and creating the career and life you want.

You are now better positioned amidst the Now Economy to be, and be known as, different and better. The next thing to consider is how we first show up in our prospective clients' lives. If we aim to show up as a highly relevant and valuable advisor, consultant, and expert, one whose ROI is significant and prominent, then the metaphorical door through which we gain entry into the lives of our clients matters a great deal. Similarly, how our prospective clients learn about what makes us different and better—our unique value proposition—also matters a great deal.

With that in mind, the next chapter will discuss the traditional means of getting new business, both warm-market and cold-market approaches, and the pros and cons of each. We are then going to introduce an alternative market, one that leverages both the strengths of warm-market and cold-market approaches while positioning us as a highly relevant and valued advisor, consultant, and expert.

ASSERTIONS

- *Predicting the future looks less like fortune-telling and more like observing the world around us looking for patterns and principles.*

- *You are no longer entitled to be in the transaction.*

- *The risk/reward ratio is a way for you to evaluate your value while giving your clients and prospective clients a different paradigm* for assessing the so-called "reward" of removing you from the transaction.

- *Creating and communicating ROI for your clients ensures that your value is well beyond the reach of big-tech industry disruption.*

REFLECTIONS

What lesson can you take and apply to your business from the disruption of the retail industry?

_____

What lesson can you take and apply to your business from the disruption of the travel industry?

_____

What is one way in which you could use the risk/reward ratio in communicating with your current or next prospective client?

_____

In what ways, and with what specific examples, could you document offering a positive ROI for your clients?

_____

How would you communicate that positive ROI regularly and naturally to current and prospective clients?

_____

3

COLD MARKET, WARM MARKET & THE NEED FOR AN ALTERNATIVE MARKET

After returning home from a church mission to Brazil, I was determined to put myself through school without going into debt or relying on help from home. I love my alma mater, and I will likely encourage all of my children to go to college. However, I will also admit that the education that I got in figuring out how to pay my way through college without any debt is even more valuable to me than the college degree that hangs in my home office today.

As I walked down the hill from the campus testing center to my apartment one night, a feeling of disappointment, anxiety, and embarrassment started to sink in. I had just failed my calculus final again. I didn't want to see or talk to anyone because I didn't have the heart to tell my roommates nor anyone in my family the news. I felt like such a loser. I had been trying to juggle classes, homework, church responsibilities, staying fit, dating, and earning an income to put myself through school. Along that walk, I remember thinking about how much time I spent working and the measly paychecks I received from my campus job and side business washing windows of homes in the surrounding area.

It was at this moment that I had an epiphany. While I could not come up with any more hours in the day, there had to be a way to spend less of those hours working while still reaching my goals. The answer was simple and clear. I just needed to figure out how to increase how much I got paid for every hour I worked.

Not long after that epiphany, I was invited to visit the nearby home of the adult couple who had overseen my group of missionaries in Brazil. Unexpectedly, and on the spot, this man and his wife offered me a job representing their mortuary, selling what was called pre-need funeral insurance. The policy that I would sell covered the costs of the insured's funeral upon their passing.

I can't say that was ever on my dream board of careers, but the way they sold it to me, the power of being in a well-paid sales profession that was flexible with all my other commitments, was convincing. In short order, I had my insurance licensing requirements, and I was selling insurance policies to the family members of the mortuary's former clients.

A cold call from a mortuary went something like this: *"Hello, this is Justin Stoddart calling on behalf of the mortuary. I'd like to set up a time to meet with you to discuss how we might be able to help you prearrange your funeral plans."*

On day one, I received a stack of papers representing "warm" leads that the mortuary figured were at higher risk of "going cold," if you know what I mean. Is this what increasing my dollar per hour looked like?

LEAD VERSUS REFERRAL

As we move further into an era of industry disruption, those industries that continue to retain space for a niche of profitable professionals include those industries which influence wealth in meaningful ways. Naturally, the professionals that will occupy those profitable niches within those industries are those that offer the leadership that best helps their clients both *preserve* and *grow* wealth.

Let me begin by making a distinction between a lead and a referral. The example below is a real estate agent talking to a lead:

Agent: Hello, is this Curt?

Curt: Who is this?

Agent: You had expressed some interest in a home over at 382 …

Curt: I'm sorry, how did you get my phone number?

Agent: You filled out a form online expressing interest in a home for sale over at …

Curt: I'm sorry to cut you off, but this is a bad time for me to talk. I don't have an interest in a home at this time, so no need to call me back. Don't call me back. I have to go. Goodbye. [click]

Agent: [thinking] Ugh … that sucked. Next phone number.

Curt was, you might say, just a little curt. If we're honest with ourselves, can we blame him? If someone were to call you out of the blue on your cell phone number, and you're not even really sure how they got your number, there's a good chance you're not going to treat them the same way you'd treat a friend or a referral from a trusted source.

This next example is a real estate agent talking to a referral:

Agent: Hello, is this Judy?

Judy: It is. With whom am I speaking?

Agent: My name is Justin, and I promised your friend Ted that I would call you. I'm his trusted real estate advisor and—

Judy: [interrupting Justin in a tone of excitement] Oh, my goodness, I'm so glad you called. Hold on just one moment, please.

[Judy speaking to someone else in the background]. Sam, that real estate advisor Ted referred to us is on the phone right now.

Justin, are you there?

Agent: Yes, I'm here.

Judy: I'm sorry to keep you waiting. I just wanted my husband to speak with you as well. We've been excited to talk with you. I'm going to put the phone on speaker now so that we can both hear you. Justin, can you still hear us?

Agent: I can hear you just fine. Thank you.

Sam: Thank you again for calling. Ted has been raving about you for so long, and we know how in demand you are. We're grateful for your time.

Agent: Ted is a good man for saying what he said. I appreciate and value his confidence.

Judy: Do you think you'd have time to come and meet with us in the next couple of weeks to help us understand what would be the best option for our family?

Now, imagine making phone calls like that regularly. They are calls that most real estate agents only dream of, and although slightly dramatized, I share it as an illustration of the difference between a "cold market" lead and a "warm market" referral.

A quick poll, which one of those two calls would you prefer to make each day? Unless you are a masochist, calling referrals is a way better option than calling leads.

Additionally, and just as importantly, the way in which you entered the lives of those prospective customers was very different. The metaphorical door through which you walk into the lives of a cold-market lead doesn't start the relationship in the best way.

On the other hand, the door you walk through when you enter into a prospect's life as a highly recommended referral is very different: you have trust and immediate credibility.

The outcome of whether or not you end up getting the business in either of those two scenarios is pretty obvious. One might even say that the distinction between a lead and a referral is the distinction between getting business via cold-market methods and getting business via warm-market methods. This is often referred to as "non-mets" and "mets." In other words, you've met the person, or you've not met the person. For simplification, I'll reference non-mets as cold-market and mets as warm-market. Let's look at the pros and cons of both methods.

Traditional Cold-Market Method

The definition of a cold-market prospecting approach is proactively making contact with people you did not know beforehand with the intent to do business with them. Now, maybe it doesn't always look like soliciting for funeral plans, but the concept is the same. In short, you are convincing someone to trust you *and* to want your product or service all at the same time.

Prospecting is a fundamental way that many real estate agents grow and sustain healthy businesses. Some examples of cold-market prospecting tactics include

- phoning expired listings,
- marketing to the neighboring homeowners around one of your listed properties, often referred to as circle-prospecting,
- door-knocking in a neighborhood, and
- calling internet leads from Zillow or some other lead source.

Cold-Market Pros
- Immediate availability to create new opportunities
- Endless supply of opportunities

- Ability to become a trusted professional in your industry for the many consumers who don't already know someone

- Easier to turn work off and enjoy time with friends and family; your clients are your clients, and your work is your work, and you don't feel the incessant need to be marketing to your friends and family when you're done for the day

Cold-Market Cons
- Low conversion rates

- Lead generation tactics not always appreciated by the consumer.

This shouldn't be a surprise to you, but lead generation tactics are not always appreciated by the consumer. In a time and era when consumer sentiment is more visible, transparent, and vital than ever before, upsetting the customer at the outset is not a healthy long-term business model.

In real estate, for example, when a listing expires, a barrage of well-intentioned agents seeking to relist the home can be infuriating to the client. Even if the agents are professional and friendly, the same phone call asking the same questions using many of the same scripts to solicit the same business can be tiring and frustrating for the homeowner.

I'll never forget the story my stepfather told me about his experience when his listing expired. He was in Europe on business and his phone just started going bonkers with incoming calls, all from agents eager to schedule an appointment to relist his home. The frequency was such that he wasn't even able to make an outgoing phone call for several hours. "Is this ever going to stop?" he wondered, "Or am I going to need to change my phone number?"

This nightmarish experience left a bad taste in his mouth, not just about the agents who called but about real estate agents in general. The professionalism of an entire industry was downgraded in his mind. He's not alone.

- Consumer responses to cold-market methods

This sort of frustration from the consumer often leads to short, curt, rude, and even obscene responses from homeowners to the professionals who are making these phone calls. When you spend your time in these types of conversations day in and day out, it can wear on you.

Traditional Warm-Market Method

I'm sure you would agree that the bread and butter of a sales and service business is referrals or business from your sphere of influence. Some would even argue that your database *is* your business.

When you think this way, you realize that your business builds on itself instead of starting over with each new lead and transaction. Don Hobbs, an early pioneer and marketing leader in the real estate industry, said it this way to an agent just getting started: *"Today, you're going to go out and try to find your first deal. If you do it right, 10 years from now, your business will come to you. If you don't do it right, you'll be out hunting for your next deal again 10 years from now."*

Said differently, some people who have been in the business for 10 years have been in business for one year, 10 different times. In other words, their business never builds on itself because they don't deepen relationships. Instead, they just go from transaction to transaction.

Warm-Market Pros

- You have pre-existing trust.

- You get to be in business with those who have been friends and family before your career began.

- You get to build relationships with those who have come into your life as a result of your career.

- Increased satisfaction by working with people you know.

- Your conversations are most often friendly and welcomed.

- Your friends, family, and past clients become tremendous leverage. Through their eyes and ears, you are able to hear more conversations and see more opportunities than you ever could on your own.

- You get to build community through client events, business mixers, and the like.

Warm-Market Cons

This model came naturally to me. I never actually questioned that there could be a problem with it until I started talking with other people, asking how it was working for them, while also evaluating how well it was working for me.

- It can be slow.

- The method doesn't often scale well. What I mean by that is that there are only so many relationships that one can be in and take care of at any given time. Even though prioritizing one's database to allocate the most amount of time to those who are most likely to refer you, the reality is that the average person from your sphere of influence is not going to come across that many referral opportunities in any given year.

- When your friends and family are also your prospects and referral sources, you may have a harder time turning work off so that you can relax.

- When your family and friends are also your clients and your referral sources, reaching out to generate new business can sometimes feel less genuine than you'd like it to feel. Not wanting to turn relationships into sales calls keeps many agents from doing the work to stay in touch. As a result, many professionals' businesses lag and struggle as a result.

In taking a closer look at cold-market and warm-market approaches, we recognize that both have their strengths and both have their weaknesses. If only there were a method that leveraged the pros of both cold-market and warm-market methods …

Mortuary Takeaways

In my time representing the mortuary, I experienced what it was like to be a solicitor. Even though I was calling families who had been clients of the mortuary previously, when I dialed them, I was showing up in their lives as a solicitor. It was a cold-market tactic to a pseudo warm market.

Most people weren't mean, but you can imagine being on the other end of that call. It must have felt a little like the Grim Reaper calling. I don't know how friendly I would have been to the mortuary calling to encourage me to make and pay for my funeral plans. Despite the discomfort, I got results. The pre-need funeral insurance agency that I worked for while representing the mortuary honored me with their Salesman of the Year award in my first year.

Side note (although an important one): the pretty girl who accompanied me to the award banquet later admitted that this award made her proud and gave her confidence in my abilities. Since that same girl agreed to marry me, one might say that her trust in me and her hand in marriage was the real award I won that evening. Additionally, she was my best and most important takeaway from this era. In addition to gaining the confidence of my future wife, I also became confident that I wanted to graduate from being a solicitor. I wanted to talk with those who wanted to talk with me and work with those who wanted to work with me. You may have had a similar experience. You gain clarity that, although you can get results this way, you don't really want to spend your career and life doing that day in and day out.

The next step in my journey gave me the opportunity to learn and utilize warm-market methods. Although I found the new job to be better than being a solicitor, I encountered firsthand the limitations and cons of these methods.

Assertions

- *Accept that there are pros and cons to growing business through cold-market strategies.*

- *Accept that there are pros and cons to growing business through warm-market strategies.*

- *Be open to the fact that there is a need for an alternative market, one that takes the pros of cold- and warm-market strategies.*

REFLECTIONS

Do you prefer growing your business through warm-market or cold-market strategies? Explain why.

___

What are the downsides for you of your preferred method?

___

How might your business and life be better if you were to learn a model that taught an alternative method that utilizes the pros of both warm- and cold-market strategies?

___

4

DISCOVERING THE UPSTREAM MODEL

"They are independent contractors!" my mom said with frustration and a hint of exasperation.

I still remember that evening around our dinner table. My parents had just received word from the IRS that their small army of 1099 independent contractors were not classified as independent contractors but as employees. Included in the IRS's notification was a near-crippling bill for back taxes and penalties.

This army of "employees" were the personnel that staffed grocery store demos—the food sampling stations like you see at Costco. What started as a small endeavor of staffing just a few demos on one weekend eventually turned into our family's primary source of income.

Growing that business was not easy and took a lot of sacrifice from our entire family. I have memories of working in our home office, making copies, packing and labeling boxes, and even having to scrap my plans on occasional Saturdays to be the fill-in product demonstrator when someone called in sick. I had been trained to greet and engage with customers coming down the grocery store aisle and offer samples of everything from kiwis, hot dogs, pizza, soda, and any other product you can imagine.

On another evening around our dinner table, my mom's eyes were notably red and puffy from crying. She shared the news that a national demo company competitor had, seemingly instantaneously, taken from us a lion share of our business.

Previously, different food manufacturers such as Kraft, Nabisco, and Pepsi had the autonomy to choose their own demo company to staff their demos. Now, this new competitor had created an exclusive agreement with a major grocery store chain that all demos in their stores were required to go through this new competitor.

In an instant, we were shut out. Our years of building relationships and offering top-tier service with hundreds of individual food manufacturers seemed to now be irrelevant. With this substantial loss in business, how would our family business survive? How would we even pay our bills?

I was unaware of what was happening to me at that time. Instead of just learning how to work in our shipping department or how to greet customers with samples, I was learning much more valuable life and business lessons. How my mom dealt with and navigated through these difficult challenges would set me up to face my own daunting future business challenges.

My Very Own General Contracting Business

Fast forward 20 years from those first business conversations around our family dinner table, and I was the owner of my own general contracting company. I had just purchased a book of business from my previous employer, who had moved his focus from high-end homebuilding to land development and needed to put all of his attention there.

Although being in business for myself came faster than I had predicted, I wasn't surprised or uncomfortable in that role. In fact, for me, it was the natural progression of getting the life I wanted, and I had grown up hearing both my parents say that if I ever wanted to get ahead, I needed to own my own business. So, there I was, 26 years old, a new wife, our first baby on the way, a four-year degree, a general contractor's license, and my very own general contracting company. I was living the dream!

In working for my previous employer, I had learned how to build a quality home and how to deal with the often tremendous expectations and demands of a high-end custom-home client. I had learned how to have the mindset, systems, and processes to remain profitable and sane. I had a strong network of subcontractors and suppliers, and together we built great homes. I felt like the world was my oyster and I was on a fast pass to massive success. The only thing between me and these big dreams was the simple task of keeping my pipeline full of new clients. Easy, right?

Although I could deliver a great finished product together with a remarkable client experience, I had misjudged one vital component of being in business for myself. I had underestimated the challenge of convincing prospective custom-home clients to entrust a kid like me with two million dollars so that I could build them their dream home.

Make special note that much of my competition had been in business as long as I had been alive. These competitors had strong brand recognition, seemingly countless past projects, and plenty of client testimonials. It may be an understatement to say that I was at a severe disadvantage.

I wanted to work by referral, but my family also wanted to eat and pay our bills that year rather than waiting until next year. Yet, the thought of soliciting for high-end custom-home clients also sounded like a bad idea. Wouldn't it be amazing if I could find a model that allowed me to work relationally while also having more control over the pace at which the business came?

This is where the Upstream Model comes in.

THE UPSTREAM MODEL DEFINED

As I shared in the introduction, the Upstream Model teaches you how to get more referrals from fewer relationships. Here is how the Upstream Model works:

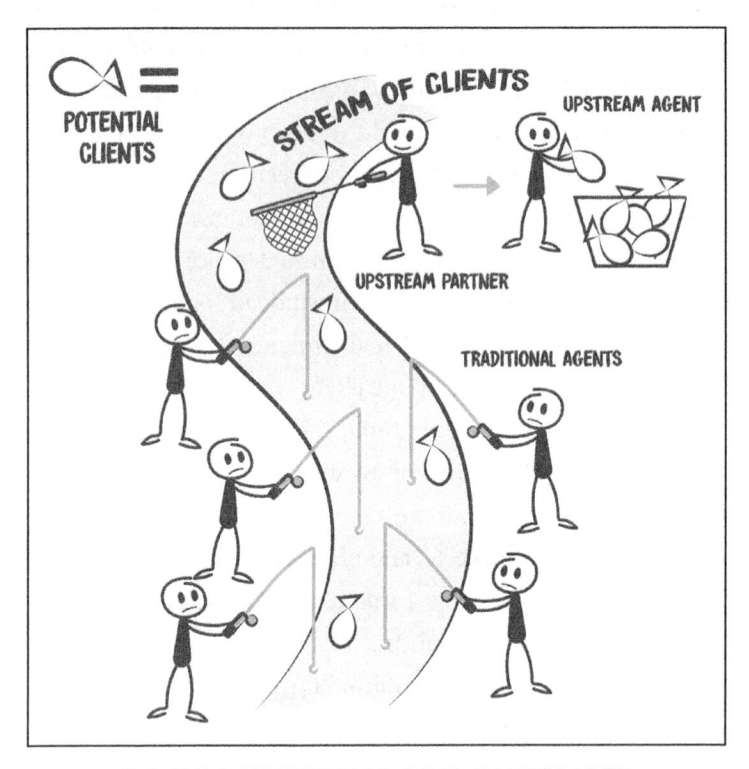

FIGURE 1: UPSTREAM MODEL ILLUSTRATED

Common warm-market methods teach you how to *personally* court hundreds of people in your database, which typically leads to only a small handful of referrals. When I say personally, I mean your primary value is *friendship*, with value as a professional coming later.

Conversely, the Upstream Model teaches you how to *professionally* court only a small handful of upstream partners in your database, which leads to hundreds of referrals. When I say professionally court, I mean your primary value is *business* value with friendship coming later.

The difference between traditional referral models and the Upstream Model is illustrated below:

TRADITIONAL MODELS

BIG DATABASE
(LOTS OF WORK AND EXPENSE) → SMALL NUMBER OF REFERRALS

UPSTREAM MODEL

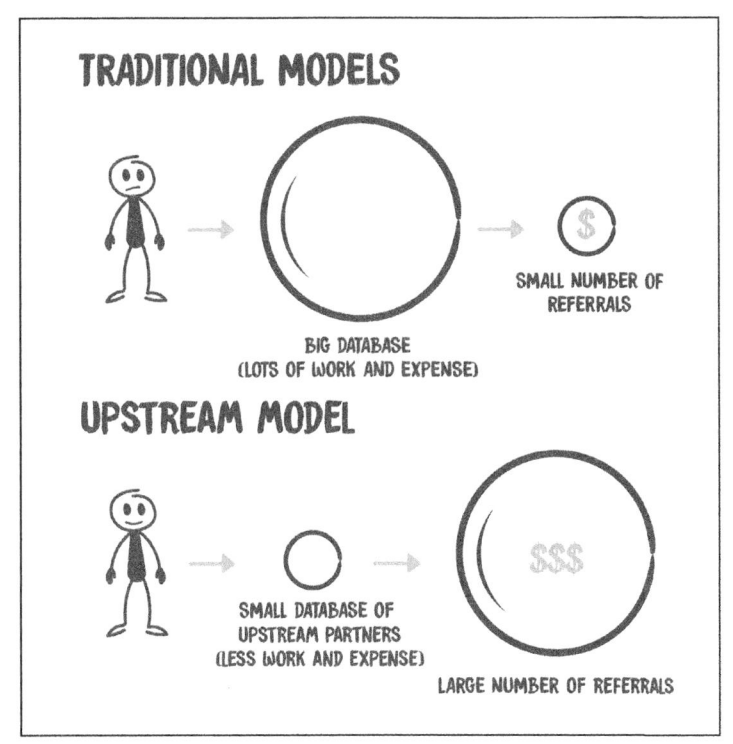

SMALL DATABASE OF UPSTREAM PARTNERS (LESS WORK AND EXPENSE) → LARGE NUMBER OF REFERRALS

FIGURE 2: UPSTREAM MODEL BENEFITS

The Upstream Model couples the pros of warm-market lead generation models (relationships) with the pros of cold-market lead generation models (scalability). Instead of a constant hunt to find the golden eggs in your market, or even in your database, you will learn how to go upstream and gain favor with the golden geese.

The Upstream Model exposes the fact that, while you may pour value into hundreds and hundreds of people, only a few of those people within that large database can and will reciprocate in the form of referrals to your business. While you spend lots of time and effort, and make a lot of friends, you will come to realize that you are reaching out to help a lot of people who can't or won't help you in return. When those relationships into which you've invested time and resources don't produce a return, or don't produce a return within the timeline that you need and want, it can be frustrating. You may even find yourself resenting individuals who, despite your best efforts, use or refer another agent.

Please don't misinterpret what I'm saying. Going into any relationship with an expectation of a return will not be genuine. Both of you will tire of inauthentic efforts to get something in return. Additionally, there's nothing wrong with making friends. There's nothing wrong with offering love, help, and service to a lot of people. In fact, that's a recipe for a really meaningful and happy life. Unless that is your sole business strategy and you go broke in the process. As probably all of us have experienced at one point in our lives, it is hard to be happy when we are worried about money.

The Upstream Model, on the other hand, helps you to recognize that there are professionals in your marketplace who are having conversations with your potential future clients before you and your competitors learn about their needs. These professionals are learning that a transaction in your industry is in these clients' future even before big tech can turn them into a lead for your competitors. By focusing your efforts on adding meaningful professional value to these upstream partners who have the ability to influence potential clients in your direction, you will gain the inside track on those who need you next.

Unlike in traditional models, these upstream partners will not refer you because they know you, like you, and trust you. Yes, that will undoubtedly happen over time; however, if that is the only reason that they are referring you, then it's too slow, inconsistent, and unreliable. Their motive must not be that they like you. Their motive must be that they need you. Their motive must be that by bringing you into the equation, they are more valuable to their clients. Only then will these referrals be natural and free flowing.

It's like applying the 80/20, or more like the 95/5 rule, to your database. When you spend more time and effort with those who can help you in more significant ways and less time with those who cannot, two things happen. First, your production goes up. Second, you gain your time back. Isn't that what all professionals want? More money *and* more time?

This strategy and these benefits are the foundation of the Upstream Model.

GOING UPSTREAM AS A HOMEBUILDER

Despite my diligent efforts to build my general contracting business solely by referral, I did not see results at the pace I needed and wanted. As I contemplated solutions for my meager pipeline, I began to ask myself this obvious question: *Who knows that a client will be building a home before that client ever talks to or chooses a homebuilder?* Or, in other words, *Who is upstream of me?*

The graphic below illustrates my position prior to applying the Upstream Model.

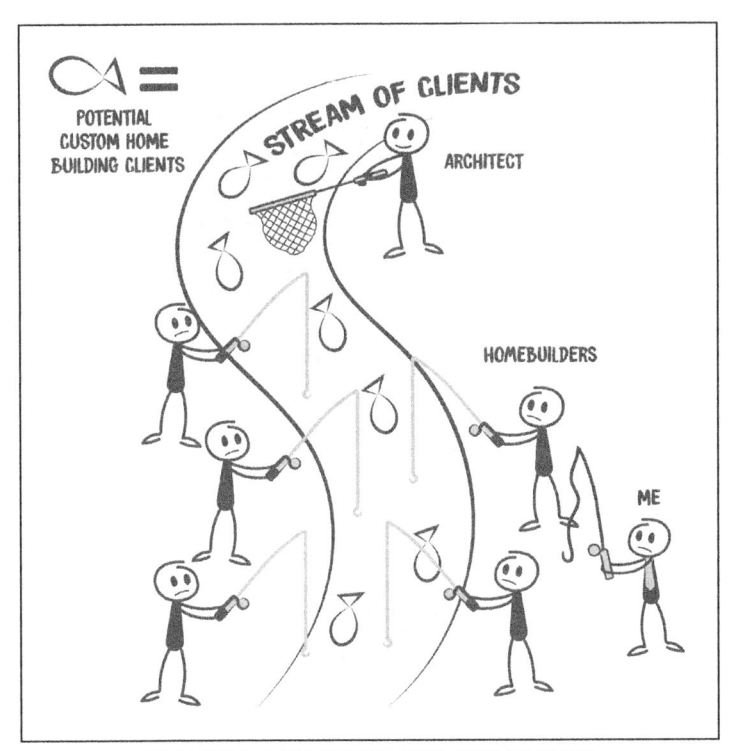

FIGURE 3: HOMEBUILDER STRUGGLES

Compare the progression of clients, from when they decide to build a home to the point when they choose a homebuilder, to that of a fish moving downstream.

If you are wondering why all the builders are fishing in the same spot, it is because they cannot bid on a project until the architectural drawings are complete. So, naturally, the builders sit right at that fishing hole with their poles in the water, eagerly awaiting the next fish to come down that stream.

These builders' piece of the shoreline represents their foothold in the marketplace. These homebuilders defended that shoreline, as they should. The better their spot along the shoreline, the more lines they could get in the water, and the more fish they could hook and reel in from that stream. Meanwhile, the homebuilder in the back represents me, trying to get my line in the water from behind the more experienced and established fishermen (and women).

My First Attempt

To get my line and bait in the water, so to speak, I walked into an architect's office, introduced myself, and dropped off some business cards. I then gave the architect my clichéd elevator pitch as to my ability to build a good home and take good care of his clients. Then, I left as if this would impress him. This strategy, however, was the common way that other builders went about getting a piece of the shoreline. It didn't take me long to realize that this wasn't going to work like I needed it to work.

Like you, I am emotionally intelligent enough to be able to read body language. From the look on someone's face, you get a pretty good idea of how that person is feeling about any given situation. At that moment, I perceived that I was not offering a solution. Instead, I was showing up in his world as a problem. I was a distraction from his ability to finish his work and keep his commitment to his paying customers. Frankly, that is not an effective way to start a relationship with one from whom I aspired to be getting referrals. As a homebuilder, I knew that architects were upstream from me and were an excellent potential source of business. I also quickly became aware that this flawed tactic put me behind others in an already very crowded fishing hole.

Looking back, that first architect's experience with me must have sounded something like this:

> *Hi, there. My name is Justin Stoddart. I wanted to stop by and introduce you to ME so that you could know all about ME, and as frequently as possible, you can send ME business.*

You see, I'm not here for any other reason than for ME. I don't care so much about your goals or even what challenges you may be struggling with. Again, I'm here for ME.

Now, I've got to go, but here are 10 of my cards so that you don't forget about ME and so that you can introduce ME to all of your clients, and so that, most importantly, you can build my business for ME.

Had I given myself a grade that day, I would have given myself a "C" for effort. However, if I were to score myself on the rest of that experience, my actual strategy once I got face-to-face, it would have been a big fat "F." I had identified a better referral source but then showed up in a way that positioned me as an in-person solicitor. Being a solicitor is undoubtedly better than sitting in your office doing nothing; however, it is not going to help you create a value proposition that protects your margins and your identity.

Remember that in the environment in which we now live and work, and the one that we're entering into, not only do we have to offer superior value but the metaphorical door through which we enter into the lives of our clients matters a great deal. The same is true when entering into the lives of those who are upstream from us.

You've heard it said that you don't get a second chance to make a first impression. Well, people are pretty smart and, believe it or not, most people cannot only listen to what you're saying but they can also read between the lines of your overall intention. For me, I was coming into this conversation with that architect with the question, *"How can I get business from this guy?"*

My Better Attempt

My next attempt at meeting with an architect was a different experience. Rather than dropping into his office unannounced, I reached out to a local, well-respected interior designer with whom I had a working relationship. I asked her if she knew a particular architect, Jared Connors. I then asked her if she'd be willing to make an introduction. I told her what to say to position me as better and different than the typical builder.

I asked her to have, in her own words, some form of the following conversation with him.

> *Hey Jared, there is a builder who you should know. His name is Justin and he builds a great home, and he works differently than other builders, which is to say his emphasis is on the client experience. As you know, many builders are not good at communicating, being transparent, being proactive, being on schedule, or being on budget. Justin really stands out in these areas. He's someone who is going to not only offer an exceptional client experience but also have a positive impact on your business as you look to continue growing in future.*

Do you see what happened before I ever met Jared in person? I did not come into Jared's world with my hands cupped like a beggar looking for a handout in a desperate attempt to have him solve my problem of not having enough business. I didn't come to "get."

On this, my "better attempt," I had a different intention. I knew that Jared could help me, but I wasn't there to make a withdrawal from an emotional bank account into which I had made zero deposits. Instead, I was there to "open an account and make my first of many deposits." With the help of someone who Jared already trusted and respected, I came into the meeting edified and pre-sold as being someone who could solve his problems *and* grow his business. I came to figure out how I could best "give" real value to Jared.

This strategy and intention got me the first appointment, and as I walked through the metaphorical door into Jared's life, it was not as a "self-serving solicitor." Instead, I leveraged the power of the third-party endorsement to be known before I was known. Doing so allowed me to influence his narrative about me and to do so with tremendous intentionality.

THE MEETING

Though the strategy of getting the appointment demonstrated that I wanted to be of unique and significant value, that alone was not enough. My strategy inside the meeting needed to be different and better as well.

My question, therefore, going into the conversation was, "What problem can I solve for Jared?"

Walking out of his office with one very tangible want or need would then allow me to focus my efforts on bringing a solution to a problem that mattered to Jared. At least in his mind, if not out loud to others, I needed him to think something to the tune of "Wow. That is not your typical builder. I'm impressed. I need to stay close to him." Keep in mind, I didn't want him to think that my real mission was "How do I get business from this guy?" I had to go into the conversation with the genuine objective of solving his problem.

Having this paradigm shift caused a shift inside me that took the pressure off a scripted performance and turned it into more of a genuine conversation in which I was seeking a way to be of value. I was now exploring how I might serve, contribute, and lead, even if in some small way, this industry partner to a better and brighter future.

When that is the genuine intention, the shift is felt on both sides of the interaction. So, what did I do during the meeting?

First, I retired the "ME conversation." This meeting wasn't about me or getting my pitch across. This meeting was about him. The interior designer had already said enough about me. It was now my time to demonstrate and reinforce that what she had said was true.

Different from warm-market methods, the Upstream Model leads with professional value, not friendship. Friendship becomes a by-product, not the leading value proposition. Nevertheless, you still must create some sort of personal connection. If I was going to commit time and effort to add value to this upstream partner, I needed to like this person and they me. I sought to make that personal connection by highlighting a few commonalities between us. When you can move a conversation beyond the cerebral and tie into the emotional, you are more likely to get buy-in from yourself and others.

An objective of the meeting was to see me not as the hero, here to "help offer value to his business." Instead, he was the hero. I was simply the guide to help him see clearly a bigger and brighter future and then to be sure that he achieved it.

Secondly, I asked two primary questions, designed to give me the insight I needed to go to work on something that mattered to him:

- As a professional, what are your most significant or most important opportunities?

- What are the biggest business obstacles or challenges you face?

As I got Jared to open up and share with me insights from these two questions, I then had the recipe for staying more relevant and more valuable than my competitors. I could show him that a faster way to his bigger goals involved me.

After the Meeting

Immediately after leaving Jared's office, I went to work on whatever opportunity or problem that I felt I could most readily address. I wanted to demonstrate that I wanted to (and could) add value.

I sent an email to Jared shortly after our meeting, not just to add value but to deliver results. I let him know that I had someone in my network who would be helpful with his big challenge. My email asked for permission to connect the two of them.

After a few more rather small efforts to bring value to Jared, something interesting happened. It always does. Jared, and subsequent architects, reached out to thank me for my efforts and to see if we could schedule a walk-through of a recent home or two that I had built.

"Why was that the request?" you ask.

Jared was impressed, and he knew that one easy way to reciprocate and add value to me was by adding me to his "approved builder list." These were builders he felt comfortable referring to his clients. If Jared saw for himself that I could build a good home and deliver for his clients like I told him I could, then he would refer me because he knew I was different than your typical builder. In short, I didn't need to fight for a piece of the shoreline. Jared was introducing me to clients before the fishing hole where my competition was hanging out.

Now, if the proverbial door through which I walked into Jared's life mattered, and it did, then so did the door through which I walked into the lives of his referred clients. Therefore, I was intentional about helping to craft the narrative used to introduce me to his clients.

In other words, I may have a spot along the shoreline and a fishing line in the water, but that does not mean that I'm automatically going to start reeling in the fish. Jared's opinion mattered, but gaining the favor of the clients themselves ultimately mattered more.

Because my youth and lack of experience put me at a disadvantage in the marketplace, I needed an endorsement and a strategic introduction that highlighted my strengths in areas where many other builders were weak. That introduction highlighted that my strengths were many other builders' weaknesses. Most builders would deliver a fine finished product; that wasn't the problem that plagued most construction projects. Instead, it was the mismanagement of budgets, schedules, and expectations, and it was overall poor communication. These common problems have created an impression that building a home is difficult. This very pain point was my opportunity to be known as someone different and better in an area that I knew my competition was too stuck in their ways to change or improve. I was fresh, innovative, and agile when my competition was not.

I seized this as an opportunity to level the playing field, not just by me saying it but by having an upstream referral partner say it. The introduction I taught Jared to use was simple.

> *There are a lot of good builders in the area, many of whose names you may recognize. I'd like to introduce you to a younger builder who I can personally verify builds a great home. Additionally, he has a real focus on the client experience.*

From this introduction, instead of being one of many, I stood out. I was the only builder who was taking a vested interest in the *businesses* of those upstream from me. Rather than being on the outside looking in, waiting years or even decades to garner enough experience, I chose to play the game differently. Some might even argue I chose to play a different game altogether, as my efforts and my strategy neutralized the advantage of my competition and even gave me the inside track. I won project after project, not because I was a more experienced or a better builder, but because I had a better model than my competitors.

Going Further Upstream

Once I realized that this approach worked with architects, I began to identify others who were even further upstream. For example, people will often contact an interior designer who helps decide what kind of home they should build and then accompanies them through the architectural design process until the house is built and furnished. And so, I began to employ similar strategies of adding value to the businesses of some interior designers.

Real estate agents selling vacant lots became another upstream referral partner, as did land developers and landowners. The further upstream I went, the less crowded it was. The downside was that these partners required me to be more patient, as introductions at that level were to people that weren't looking to build a home for several years. However, I discovered that those furthest upstream became a real value-add for my more immediate upstream referral partners.

As an example, helping Jared solve some of his biggest challenges included helping him to fill his pipeline with new clients. I did this by introducing him to a real estate agent who specialized in selling empty lots ready for homebuilding. While selling a building lot, the real estate agent was able to get Jared involved early so that his clients knew what kind of home they could design on a particular lot. Having Jared involved early in the process not only improved the real estate agent's client experience but also helped the real estate agent to sell more building lots, and to do so quicker and more easily than he could without having Jared present. Naturally, the agent wanted Jared involved, and so Jared became the first in line to receive introductions and referrals from this agent, which of course, helped him to fill his pipeline.

The two most beautiful things about all of this:

1. The value that Jared now received from this agent became part of my value proposition to Jared.

2. It wasn't that hard.

I would identify these further upstream partners by going back to the critical upstream question: *Who else knows that a home will be built before that client talks to a builder?* Or, *Who knows that a home will be designed before that client talks to an architect?*

As I identified these further upstream referral partners, I applied the same principles I already deployed to get an appointment, act on takeaways from the meeting, and then follow through after the meeting. As I did this, more and more opportunities began to present themselves, and my value proposition became more robust and my spot along the shoreline upstream from the competition became more secure.

I knew that while most builders were approaching architects, they were doing so using an ineffective strategy. The strategy was lazy and self-serving and did not take into account the needs and concerns of the architect. For this reason, it was a slow and arduous process for them to begin getting the architect's referrals and endorsement.

Additionally—and this is critical—if by chance there was a builder both intuitive and savvy enough to ask, listen, and even write down the challenges of the architect, the builder's approach to bringing value to the architect all centered around bringing value from within his role as a builder. It would be value based solely on building a better home or offering a better client experience.

I stood out by being able to not just deliver on creating a better client experience but by also bringing value from outside the homebuilding silo. This approach is uncommon (if not unique) and creates a space where your competition becomes less and less relevant, and your margins and identity get stronger and stronger.

A Return to the Family Dinner Table

After my mom's tears dried from having lost most of our customers in one day, she knew we were watching and learning. Keep in mind, my mom doesn't cuss very often, so when she does, you better watch out. I'll never forget the fire that came back into her eye as she spoke up and said:

> *"This is not over yet. That company is not going to come in here and take what I've worked so hard to build. To hell with them."*

Rather than trying to piece her business back together with a few demos here and there from smaller vendors and at smaller retailers, she knew she needed a better model. She discovered that her new, most significant sources of business were the decision-makers at grocery chains so that she could compete for a similar exclusive agreement. She had to go upstream.

It wasn't long before she had managed to add such value to these upstream partners that they replaced the other national agency with our company. She then repeated her steps and did the same thing with another large grocery retailer.

As a result of her discovery and application of this model, she led our little family business, serving many retailers, manufacturers, employees, and communities, for 27 years. At its peak, she had over 1000 demos happening every weekend in stores in four states.

Without adopting this new model, disruption in her industry would have forced my mom to own an unprofitable business that wore out her health and her relationships, or become a lower-paid functionary/customer service representative of one of these national demo agencies, or forced her out of her industry altogether. Instead, the outcome she produced served a multitude of people very well for almost three decades.

Her outcome continues to benefit many more people every day. Not only have I applied it throughout my career, I'm now sharing it with you and many others. Like my mom, we have the choice to take what disruption serves us and adjust our appetite for success, or with a bit of fire in our eye, we too can say *"To hell with them"* and begin applying the principles of the Upstream Model to go on to creating a life of even greater success.

The Upstream Model brought my mom tremendous business success, but it also gave her much more than that. It also allowed her to create a life of significance. By allowing her to focus her efforts on a small database of the right upstream partners who created a massive number of referrals, she wasn't consumed by her business. She was able to have a successful business and a life. She used that time to pour deeply into the lives of her children, her friends, and other people and causes that were in need. Her deep involvement in my life, in the lives of my siblings, and the lives of countless people who have been blessed by her love, example, and radiance would not have happened without her discovery and application of the Upstream Model.

In the next chapter, we will take a look at how to apply the Upstream Model in your industry. This model will be critical in offering you additional help to protect and grow your margins, your business, and your professional reputation and identity so that you can live, give, and serve abundantly.

ASSERTIONS

- *Upstream partners exist who know your prospective client before your potential client ever talks to you or your competition.*

- *When professionals from your industry identify these upstream partners, they show up as solicitors or vendors.*

- *As you learn the strategies and tactics of the Upstream Model, you will stand out and your upstream partners will want to refer business to you.*

- *As you apply this model, you'll find yourself in a profitable space that your competition neither knows exists nor knows how to find.*

REFLECTIONS

How might your business and life look different if you were to have a few upstream partners that endorsed and referred you very regularly?

Have you ever engaged in the "ME conversation" with an upstream referral partner? Why was it ineffective?

_____

Have you ever had someone come into your office and offer the "ME conversation"? What did it trigger in you?

_____

What are some upstream referral industries in your sector?

_____

Who are some specific upstream professionals you could approach this week?

_____

What are some questions you could ask that would start things off on the right foot?

_____

5

THE UPSTREAM MODEL APPLIED TO YOU

"Steve, it's Justin. It's been a long time. How are you?"

In that familiar brotherly tone, he replied, "Hey, Jus! It's great to hear from you."

Steve had been my brother's best friend through childhood and in college, and he was best man at my brother's wedding. My mom, to this day, still says he's "one of my kids." Steve had become like a second older brother to me and hearing him call me that same nickname that he had used from years past triggered a feeling of assurance.

Assurance was something I needed at the time because, frankly, I was struggling. As a result of the Global Financial Crisis of 2008, the construction industry had taken a complete and utter nosedive. The net worth of many of my high-end homebuilding clients and prospective clients had been cut in half within just a few short months. My growing pipeline began to dry up as I learned that potential client after potential client was putting their construction project plans on hold until things improved.

It was a dark time in the real estate industry, and my mentors predicted that it would be five years until the industry recovered. Looking back, they were right.

Had I been passionate about developing land and building homes, I would have taken a different strategy. I would have cut my expenses, leaned further into my relationships with my upstream partners and unlike most high-end homebuilding businesses during that time, I would have survived. Instead, I decided to finish out our existing projects and close operations for my company both in Utah and then later in Texas. Working outside of the real estate industry for the next several years gave me the time, space, and experience to discover that my passion was developing people instead of land and building businesses instead of homes.

Seeking a career that aligned with this passion was what prompted my call to Steve. Steve had a history of being one of the most well-connected people that I knew, not to mention a successful real estate agent and leader of multiple real estate offices.

"I'd love to meet up and pick your brain a bit. I'm ready to do something different in my career, and I'd love to know if there's someone in your network who I should know," I said.

"Are you looking for a job?!" he said.

His tone sounded as if he was surprised. Having been around my family since childhood, Steve knew that I had been raised by entrepreneurial parents, that I had learned from an ambitious older brother, and that I had run and grown businesses of my own. As he was searching to confirm if this was indeed the motivation for my call, I too was searching inside my own soul to try to answer this question for myself.

Looking for a job felt like such a cop-out to my entrepreneurial aspirations and DNA. At that moment, my ego would have preferred to tell Steve how great I was doing and how I didn't need a thing in the world. Yet, that wasn't my reality. I had stewardship to provide for my wife, and at the time, four kids. I subtly confirmed that this was an option to which I was open and kept listening.

"I was just hired to be the sales manager for a title and escrow company. If you're looking for a job, I'd love to hire you. The problem is that I can't see you as a title and escrow sales executive. I think you would do well in my job as the sales manager. However, I'm pretty sure I'm going to like my job, so I'm not going to let you have it," he said jokingly.

I appreciated Steve's comment as it softened the blow to my ego and helped to alleviate my inner struggle. Steve had always had a gift of reading people and making them feel like they belonged. I appreciated this about him in this moment almost as much as I had 25 years earlier when I was the new kid in a new middle school.

After our call, I reached out to my stepmom, a real estate agent herself, to ask about the title and escrow industry. Before I could get the question out of my mouth, she replied, "Oh, Sweetheart. You don't want to do that. I know you, and I know what title sales executives do, and trust me, that's just not a good fit for you. You'd be so bored. Let me tell you what those people do. They come into my office, distract us, and then they try to schmooze us and take us to lunch. I just don't have time for that. I've used the same person for my title work for fifteen years, and a sales executive has never influenced that decision."

Her description helped explain why neither she nor Steve could see me in that role.

Several months passed before Steve and I made time to meet. Something had changed in between when we first talked and when we sat down to meet. He had changed his tone. He wanted to talk about the opportunity of me being a sales executive for his title and escrow company. You can imagine my confusion at that moment. Either Steve now thought less of me, or his perspective on the opportunity had changed. I like to think it was the latter of the two, but only he knows for sure.

He went on to share how, in his years of running real estate agent offices, a key priority had been working with the highest producing agents in his offices. While those top agents had needs, concerns, and problems, it had become increasingly clear to him that the traditional title sales executive was unequipped to identify and solve the more significant issues of those agents. And only in solving those bigger problems could one get the attention away from their existing title and escrow relationships.

Despite what he had previously believed, with my background of having owned and run multiple businesses, Steve now saw an opportunity for me. He saw something that he didn't see before. He believed I could come in, disrupt the status quo value proposition of the title and escrow industry, and convert business from these top agents.

Steve and his company made me an offer that I accepted with this caveat in mind: "For the time being, I'll take this job, continue to expand my network, and then I'll continue looking for a role that is in alignment with my passion."

This appeased both the stewardship of providing for my family and my entrepreneurial aspirations. My decision to see this as an interim job while I decided what business I was going to either buy or start received reinforcement during my first few weeks on the job. I quickly discovered that the more talented and productive the real estate agents were, the less interest they had in meeting with me.

After the first few stiff arms, I began to feel like I was showing up in their world, trying to solve a problem they had already solved. Instead of being a solution, I was now a problem! I was distracting them from their most important work. I was a solicitor, or at best, just another vendor.

I began to have flashbacks of my first visit to that architect's office. Here I stood, once again, with my fishing pole in hand, just downstream from the top real estate agents with whom I wanted to be in business. I was trying to get close enough to the stream to get my line in the water along a very crowded shoreline.

Considering my current situation, I felt a touch of anxiety about my concern for providing for my wife and four children. More frequently than I care to admit, my stepmom's warning echoed in my ears: "Oh, Sweetheart. You don't want to do that."

To make something of my new career choice, I knew that I was going to have to tap into my best thinking and strategies. Not only would the Upstream Model prove to be my path forward for building a sizable and loyal book of business in the title and escrow industry, but it would also prove to be a profitable path forward for my real estate agent and mortgage loan officer upstream partners amidst an increasingly competitive and disruptive era.

WILL IT WORK FOR ME?

Now that I enjoy the privilege of reaching and serving professionals from a myriad of professional industries through my coaching, consulting, mentoring, and media efforts, I often get asked, "Will the Upstream Model work for me?"

My answer to that question is "yes" if you can relate to any of the following:

- As one responsible for bringing revenue into your company, you feel a constant desire and pressure to perform. Your business, your teammates, your family, and your future depend upon you making it happen day in and day out.

- You're watching as technology disruptors in the service sector get better every day at getting and keeping the attention of your clients. You recognize that when your clients repeatedly look to a source other than you for information and guidance, at least two threats show up in your business:

    § Your future opportunities are fewer because the disruptors intercept your client relationships by taking your customers or introducing them to your competitors.

    § Your margins are squeezed by these disruptors because you are either buying leads from them, sharing commissions with them, or spending more marketing dollars and effort to keep your clients' attention from them.

- You wonder what this trend means for you and your future. While you don't have bandwidth to give much attention to this threat of industry disruption, you also believe that it shouldn't go totally ignored.

- You hope and trust that as long as you focus on strategies that encourage and empower you to be more relevant, more timely, more valuable, and more relational to your sources of business and their referrals, you'll remain well-paid and at the center of the transaction.

Regardless of your specific industry, if any of the above resonate with you, then I can attest that applying the Upstream Model into your business will be of great benefit to you.

FOUNDATIONAL PRINCIPLES

The first step we must all take to begin applying the Upstream Model into our businesses is to embrace two foundational principles. Embracing these principles will position us for being able to the next steps of identifying the who and the how.

1. Stop being a solicitor and a vendor

I deserved the lack of results and negative feedback I got in my first few weeks of being a title sales executive. Although it was clear who our upstream referral partners were, the proverbial door through which I walked into the world of real estate agents and mortgage loan officers was that of a solicitor or vendor at best. I had not yet thought through or applied the Upstream Model principles I learned in previous businesses. Real estate agents and mortgage loan officers can relate to a title sales executive coming at you using an ineffective model. There is no shortage of them. Before I wised up, that was me.

Maybe you've tried to go upstream before, and perhaps you have had an experience similar to my first few weeks in title. For example, you hear from a reputable source that attorneys, or CPAs, or you name it, are all good referral sources. So, you network into one and the "ME conversation" that I introduced in Chapter 4 ensues.

If you have *never* done anything like this, whether in someone's physical office or their email inbox, then you are ahead of most of us. If you have done, even one line from the "ME conversation," then I'd like to ask you the following questions:

- How effective was it?
- Did you get any referrals?
- Did it strengthen your relationship with that upstream partner?

If you're like most people on the other end of that conversation, those business cards do not make it into the hands of clients. Instead, they get filed away, and often that file is the wastebasket under the desk. More importantly, we may consciously, or even subconsciously, make a mental note that says: *Although I respect the proactivity of that "professional," he or she is there to get a transaction, not build a relationship. This individual is out of touch with me and, therefore, may also be out of touch with any referrals I could send his or her way. He or she has just ensured that they would never get any referrals from me.*

Although this may seem harsh for someone out hustling, the reality is that a self-serving solicitor is not someone we want to introduce to our clients. Additionally, just as you and I both barely have time to keep up with all of the demands of our own businesses, we definitely don't have time to take on the sales and marketing role pro bono for some solicitor or vendor who just stepped into our office unannounced. Especially when this visitor, whether it be in your physical office or even your email inbox, has no interest or skill in discovering any of your problems, let alone being a solution to any of them. Does this remind you of my encounter with that first architect? Was I there to bring a solution to him? Do you think one of his biggest concerns was having someone to whom he could refer business? Probably not.

2. Don't solve problems that are already solved

In respect of my role as a title sales executive, does solving a real problem for top agents and mortgage loan officers look like showing up to give them another escrow officer when the one they use has served them at a high level for years?

- Does it look like giving them another number to call to access the same reports that they're already getting from a competitor?

- Does it look like loading another app on their phone that is similar to the apps from other title companies?

- Does solving a real problem look like showing up to be friends or take them out for lunch?

Are not enough apps, not enough friends, or the inability to buy their own lunch among the biggest problems that top real estate agents and mortgage loan officers are facing? It's kind of funny when you step back and look at an ineffective model. It becomes clear why it hasn't given us the results we had hoped for.

Whether you're in title insurance, commercial or residential real estate, property and casualty insurance, life insurance, financial advisement, or any other well-paid professional industry, our approach is often the same. We go at our potential customers and referral sources trying to solve our problem of not having them as a customer by offering to solve a problem that they've already taken care of. When we do this, *we become the problem* because we're wasting the time of this potential upstream partner.

In my new role, it didn't take long for me to identify that it was entirely commonplace for title reps to go upstream to get business from real estate agents. It was just as typical for a sales executive to show up and solve a problem that was already solved. What was *uncommon* was for a sales executive to come into the relationship introduced by someone who already had a strong rapport with the upstream partner. Then, armed with great questions and seeking to know the real estate agent or mortgage loan officer's biggest concerns, challenges, and problems, he or she would sit down with one sole focus: *"What problem can I solve for this agent/loan officer that they have not already solved?"*

The first and most common answer that I quickly discovered came as no surprise, which was that they were in constant pursuit of generating sufficient leads and referrals. In short, it was the first focus of every business—attracting clients so that they would then have the opportunity of serving those clients.

It started to become clear that business is business. Meaning that I was, and am, trying to solve very similar problems in my business to those my customers were, and are, trying to solve in their businesses. Revenue is the lifeblood of any business. That should be prominent in all our minds, and when in doubt, revenue generation is always a problem to solve.

While I was applying the Upstream Model in my title business, I began to see the relevance and application of real estate agents using it in their businesses as well. In other words, an effective way for me to add value to my upstream referral partners was to teach them the principles of the Upstream Model.

This strategy will also serve you well.

To become a solution to their problem, I was teaching them this fundamental question: *Who knows that someone is going to buy or sell real estate before that person ever talks to a real estate agent?*

The answer to this question led me down an inspiring path for both the individual agents whom I serve, as well as for the industry as a whole.

It was a path that, if done correctly, would weekly, if not daily, have other trusted professionals uncovering referral opportunities for agents from the conversations that they were already having with their clients.

WHO IS UPSTREAM FROM YOU?

As an example, the question "Who is upstream from me?" is answered by answering the upstream question: *Who else knows that a home will be bought or sold before that client ever talks to a real estate agent?*

There are two broad categories of people upstream from a real estate agent. First is the *blue-collar* category. I was blind to this opportunity until agent after agent told me that some of their best referral sources came from painters who would ask the homeowner, "Why are you painting your home? Are you planning to stay in the home, or are you preparing it to sell?"

Of course, if they said they were selling, that blue-collar professional was in a prime position to say, "Have you already spoken with a real estate agent? I know a great one who people just love."

Additional examples include the flooring contractor, landscaper, kitchen remodeler, or roofing contractor who would ask some version of the same question to their clients. These are the businesses that people hire before putting their home on the market, so these people can become a powerful resource to agents.

Unrelated to contractors who do direct work on a house are other potential resources. I have interviewed agents who have had tremendous success with hairstylists! It sounds odd, but hairstylists have their clients in the chair for hours, talking about all kinds of topics, including real estate. Believe it or not, these stylists could be some of the very first to know about an upcoming house move!

My point with mentioning blue-collar professionals here isn't to make a comprehensive list, but rather to open your mind to identifying people from any of a myriad of industries that can help you to answer the upstream question. Remember: knowing a great "who" can quickly be of no value if not correctly approached. So don't forget what you've learned in previous chapters.

The second category is *white-collar*. Think financial advisors, insurance agents, CPAs, tax advisors, real estate attorneys, family law attorneys, mediators, and so on. Compared to that of the blue-collar group, I have found this group to be more of an untapped and overall better opportunity for a couple of reasons:

- This group tends to be more challenging in terms of offering value and not at the top of mind for a real estate agent because they have less directly to do with a real estate transaction. As a result, fewer agents approach these professionals. Additionally, this group tends to be more sensitive to solicitors who show up to solve a problem that is already solved. As a result, agents trying this route often burn that bridge before they get to cross it.

- This group spends their career building deep trust with their clients. Their per hour rate is typically higher than the blue-collar group. Naturally, if the marketplace compensates someone at a higher rate than another, we as consumers are validating with our dollars that the value they bring to us is worth more to us. Their insights, thus, tend to be trusted more. When their insights are trusted more, their recommendations of a real estate agent or mortgage loan officer often carry more weight than those coming from a painter, as an example.

Keep in mind that the goal isn't to walk into a professional's office and walk out with a referral. That will happen, but we are farming, not hunting. No one likes being hunted, and they especially don't want a hunter going after their clients. Their job is to protect their clients from hunters, not offer them up to them.

Your goal from your very first encounter, both with blue-collar and with white-collar upstream partners, should revolve around this question: *What problem can I solve for this [specify professional] that they have not already solved?*

This mindset now positions you as a solution and a faster path to the fulfillment of their goals. Additionally, it triggers their internal dialog that says: *"Wow, this real estate agent is different than the others I know."*

UPSTREAM PARTNERS

For your offer to trigger a positive reaction in your upstream partners, they have to see you as being different. So, first things first: the way you find and approach that person must be different than showing up as a typical solicitor or vendor with your hand out. As taught previously, being aware and strategic about the door through which you walk into someone's life matters.

Showing up pre-sold and edified from someone who knows the upstream partner helps. It may even be someone with whom you already have a relationship and trust. Here are some additional tips, looking at the example of a real estate agent.

1. The right upstream partners

Part of finding the right upstream partner will depend upon with whom you are able to reach and connect. Additionally, here are a few characteristics I've found to be common among those upstream partners that have been a good fit for me as well as for those that I serve and lead:

- High character: you need to be able to believe and trust what your upstream partner tells you.

- High competence: you must have a partner who knows what they're doing and offers a high and consistent level of service to their clients.

- Coachable: you want someone who is open to receiving help and following a model.

- Strong future: you must have someone who isn't so close to the end of their career that they are in cruise control, uninterested in continuing to add new value and grow their practice.

2. Finding your upstream partners

The most straightforward way to go about this is to look around to see who you already know. It is totally possible that you don't yet have the right people in your network. Or, you might not have carried yourself in such a way that these professionals see you as being different than the average professional in your industry.

For example, you may have already engaged with this professional using a short-sighted tactic like handing them a stack of your business cards in a typical solicitor kind of way. You may feel that it would be challenging for them to see you differently now. In this situation, it may make sense for you to find a professional with whom you have not yet met. You may want a fresh start to create a first impression that can trigger that you are different and more valuable than the typical professional in your industry.

One of the best ways to get a referral to an upstream partner is to call or email your clients to let them know the following:

- As you know, we are always seeking ways to add value to our trusted clients.

- Many of the clients that we have the privilege of serving do not have all of the trusted relationships in place that would best serve the fulfillment of both their short-term and long-term goals.

- When we see an opportunity to make an introduction that would fill a gap for one of our clients, we want to be able to make an introduction that adds value to our clients.

- The introductions that we anticipate making, for example, include CPAs, financial advisors, insurance agents, tax accountants, estate attorneys, etc.

- As one of our existing clients, we have the utmost respect for you, and we trust that the people and professionals with whom you associate are similar in caliber to you and your family.

- Are there any professionals within those industries that you believe we should consider meeting and referring to our other clients?

By communicating this series of points to your clients, you've done a few things:

- You have created a touchpoint with a client.

- You have reminded your client what makes you different from other real estate agents.

- You have shared that your value proposition to your clients is getting even better.

- You're going to get a referral to a professional that will not be cold.

3. Connecting with your upstream partners

Once you have the name of a financial advisor, for example, you can now reach out and make contact. If you were to call in cold, the professional would have very little to lose in saying, "No, thank you." Whereas in a referral situation, by declining you, this professional risks offending the referral source. The stakes go up, and there is a higher likelihood that they are going to meet with you. You have avoided the cold call while benefiting from the trust that already existed between these two parties. So don't mess it up by acting like a solicitor.

4. Creating your value proposition (NB, It's not just your referrals that matter)

In the previous chapter, I outlined an example of how that first meeting can look. After that, there is a lot of value in identifying additional ways that you can be of value to your upstream referral partners. I'm going to use the financial advisor as an example going forward, but you could insert in any other upstream partner.

I have interviewed dozens of wealth managers on what would be of value to them. They are, of course, interested in the referrals that can come from the conversations you have with your clients (discussed above). However, what is even more interesting to them are your added value propositions.

VALUE PROPOSITIONS

A. Enhancing their client experience

This is the simplest and quickest impact that you can have on a financial advisor.

We designed wording that I used above to ask for a referral *to* an upstream partner from your existing clients to trigger in their heads that you are uncommon and more valuable than the typical real estate agent. Similarly, this financial advisor seeks to trigger the same response in the minds of his clients that he is more valuable than the status quo professional in his industry.

Just as the stereotype for a real estate agent is *All they want to do is sell your home or sell you a home*, the stigma for a financial advisor is this: *All they want to do is sell you more insurance and investments.*

This stigma applies to those in any industry that suffers with having "commission breath." When a professional has not yet paid the price to produce at a high enough level, and they need a deal to close so that they can take care of their own needs, their ability to think on behalf of their client as a true fiduciary is often clouded.

As a result of this stigma, financial advisors, for example, are looking for ways to show their clients that they are holistic advisors, not just a pusher of financial products. Here's one way for you to help them do this. Strong financial advisors have regular reviews. Typically, this is an annual phone call or meeting. It could be a quarterly review for large, complex financial portfolios or every other year for a client with a small or simpler portfolio. In those meetings, a financial advisor is typically giving the clients some sort of update on the market and how the client's specific investments have performed. They're also asking questions about the clients' life plans and goals. From the answers they receive, they're evaluating whether or not it makes sense to make any adjustments to their overall plan.

Some financial advisors bring up the topic of real estate in those conversations, while others do not. Those who do bring up real estate, and can talk about it with timely market data, improve their status in the eyes of their clients. How powerful, then, would it be for a financial advisor to come equipped to that meeting with a few talking points about real estate specific to where this particular client owns properties? How powerful would it be for this financial advisor to come prepared with a simple comparative market analysis of their clients' real estate portfolio?

Imagine if a financial advisor, or one of their staff members, could reach out to you or one of your staff members in advance of these client review meetings to retrieve that customized, relevant, and valuable data to use as talking points with their clients. Imagine how beneficial that could be for these upstream partners in adding more value to their clients, enhancing the client experience, and defying the stigma that they are only there to push more financial products.

As I've spoken with financial advisors about this collaboration, three key motivators have emerged:

1. It would be extremely valuable to the financial advisor and their clients.

2. It would endear the real estate agent who is offering this data to the financial advisor.

3. It would position this real estate agent as paramount in the advisor's mind upon discovering a particular client has any real estate goals.

The data that you, as a real estate agent, swim in all day long would set your upstream partners apart and help them to solve one of their biggest challenges and concerns: *How do I enhance my client experience and defy the stigma of just being a pusher of financial products?*

B. Keeping their clients "on plan"

When a client has real estate needs and goals, by positioning yourself to work with the financial plan in mind, or even together with the financial advisor, you become an invaluable partner.

Once a financial advisor has developed a plan that aligns with the core desires of that particular client, the biggest challenge they face is keeping that client "on plan." There are a couple of reasons why this happens.

Consumerism. As a whole, the world's population is more prosperous than ever. With this increase in wealth comes a seemingly endless supply of widgets, gadgets, and options for comfort, leisure, and entertainment. Not only are the products better and more attractive than ever before but advertising is more seductive, and the number of mediums through which advertisers can reach us is unprecedented. Consumerism may not seem like a problem unless the value that you bring to the marketplace is centered around helping people live a good life *and* build wealth; consumerism can get in the way of the latter.

Competing advisors. Through these same advertising channels also come offers for robo-advisors and other financial advisement options. Whether it be that or the voices and offerings of human competitors, financial advisors are always trying to retain their clients.

While some would argue that the rise of robo-advisors is a good thing for consumers, I would say that it is a bit of a crapshoot as to whether a financial product makes sense unless assessed through the lens of a particular client's unique goals and their plan to achieve those goals.

As a real estate agent or other professional evaluating another upstream partner's problem, you may be asking, *"How am I supposed to help retain a financial advisor's clients?"*

In this example, merely having a co-advisor in their life (you) is valuable. You become the ally of the financial advisor. You become aware of the client's plan when appropriate, united in helping that client to reach their biggest goals and then reinforcing the merits of the financial advisor and their plan when that advisor is not present. That is extremely valuable.

C. Reciprocal value

Maybe you've already jumped ahead in your mind about the many possibilities that open when real estate comes up in a conversation between a financial advisor and their clients. This professional has dedicated their life to becoming trained, educated, and informed to do well by their clients. They have spent years, if not decades, as a trustworthy steward and fiduciary of their clients' most important financial plans. This financial advisor, now endeared to you, will be meeting each of their clients for a financial review. In that meeting, they will be asking their clients as part of that holistic review if they plan on making any changes to the real estate portion of their total financial picture.

At the very instant when the advisor would most likely be learning of an opportunity to refer, they will be using talking points given by you. You will have positioned yourself as the financial advisor's go-to person in all things real estate. You will have situated yourself to be able to have them generate pre-qualified referrals for you from within their database on a very regular basis.

Said differently, you have helped this financial advisor to serve clients from their existing client base at an even higher level, while simultaneously opening the door to attracting more clients for your own business. That's a powerful place to be.

Opportunities to reciprocate will naturally begin to show up:

- When you transition your practice toward that of being more than just a real estate agent who can market and sell homes

- When you think like and adopt methods similar to that of a strong financial advisor, as you take on the role of being a financial advisor over your clients' real estate portfolios

- When you consider the non-real-estate data points that you could get from a financial advisor that would allow you to offer an elevated experience for your clients

Now the roles are reversed. You can serve your clients at an even higher level, while simultaneously opening the door for the advisor to attract more clients for their business.

Why They Are Not Referring You

This question often comes up: if financial advisors, estate attorneys, CPAs, and so many others know that a real estate transaction is going to happen, why aren't they referring it to a real estate agent? That's a great question.

I have interviewed dozens of financial advisors, and our conversations have gone similarly to the following script.

> **Me**: Is it true that during regular financial review meetings with clients you uncover the fact that they have a real estate transaction in their future?
>
> **Advisor**: Yes.
>
> **Me**: Frequently or infrequently.
>
> **Advisor**: Pretty frequently.

Me: Are you referring those clients to a real estate agent?

Advisor: No.

Me: Why not?

The answer is not because they don't know one. According to the National Association of Realtors, the average consumer knows between 11 and 12 agents. There must be some other reason.

I was given one interesting answer that has given me insight as to why the gap exists between a known opportunity and a referral passed. It also gave me insight as to how an agent can reposition themselves, their conversations, and their value proposition differently to cause advisors to bring them in. To the question, the answer came: *"I am not referring a real estate agent because, unlike them, I do not have past clients. I just have clients."*

Digging deeper into this answer, I discovered that financial advisors see themselves working very differently than real estate agents. They have clients for life, not just for a transaction. Their only "past clients" are clients that are no longer their clients.

Advisors, whether consciously or subconscious, question a real estate agent's ability to influence these referrals in a significant way. Additionally, there is a risk of referring an agent who has some chance of messing up the transaction or not having the highest level of client care. If that's the risk, and the benefit is only the value you can bring to that client in just a few months' worth of service, then the risk isn't worth the reward.

Within this topic of past clients versus no past clients there is a lot of opportunity for you to be seen and positioned very differently than your competition, including your big technology competitors. As you do, you will be able to tap into this potential gold mine of opportunity for you that financial advisors are unearthing in their databases. I go into this in more depth in the additional resources I provide at *upstreammodel.com*.

OH, SWEETHEART (REVISITED)

One year after I received that warning from my stepmom about being a title sales executive, she called me with some encouraging words. She had now also become a client of mine, leaving behind her prior fifteen year relationship to support me.

She said, "Justin, I have to tell you, you've really built a reputation for yourself. We just had a conversation with the person I've used for years, and the whole industry is talking about you. You've done this role of title sales executive different than anyone else in your industry. You ought to be really proud of yourself."

She was sitting next to my dad with her phone on speaker when she made that call. Being acutely familiar with the pressure that is upon a father of a young family, my dad piled on with more proud words of praise and encouragement. What once were feelings of anxiety were now replaced by feelings of gratitude and accomplishment.

I'm sure that as you got started in your industry, you too had people give you the same warning that I had received: "Oh, Sweetheart, you don't want to be a [...]. I know what those people do."

To this day, you may still have some who can't see you succeeding in that role. Don't be upset at them, and don't buy into their narrative. I'm sure they love you and want the best for you, but they've likely seen dozens of others with poles in hand, desperately trying to get their line in the water along a very crowded shoreline.

What these loved ones don't know and can't yet see is you going upstream, applying the principles, strategies, and tactics discussed to offer significant value to upstream partners. They cannot yet see how doing so will allow you to help your partners to provide an elevated client experience to their clients, causing them to want to bring you into the conversation with their clients. They can't see how this will open the door to an abundance of quality referrals in which you are pre-sold and edified as an expert. They can't yet see how this will allow you to maintain strong margins and a strong work-life balance, all by getting more and better referrals from fewer relationships.

What they also cannot yet see is that while the typical professional in your industry sits in the crosshairs of industry disruption, spending their efforts touting their ability to do that which algorithms and artificial intelligence can or will soon be able to do, you are positioning yourself differently. As an upstream professional yourself, you will bring such value that upstream partners will line up to refer you, clients will line up to use you, and those clients will see to it that you remain well-paid and at the center of their transaction so that they get the benefit of the high value that you have to offer.

This scenario will become your reality as you continue to learn and apply the principles of the Upstream Model, becoming an upstream professional.

To harness the full potential of this model, it is important to have the right mindset, intentions, strategies, and tactics. I was unable to include all of that in this book, so I've created and made available additional resources for you at *upstreammodel.com*.

In our next chapter, I share how, in the eyes of your upstream partners, you can quickly and intentionally advance from being a solicitor or mere vendor to being a peer. Then, I will teach you, using very intentional and specific strategies, how to move from being just a peer to being a mentor and leader. As you make this progression, you will become an invaluable part of their business and a natural referral to their clients.

ASSERTIONS

- *Your best clients will lead you to your best upstream referral partners.*

- *As a service industry professional, it doesn't take much to stand out in the eyes of upstream referral partners.*

- *The real opportunity with upstream partners is becoming an enhancement to their client experience.*

- *Doing so opens the door for you to be introduced regularly.*

REFLECTIONS

Who is an upstream referral partner for you?

___

Would you consider yourself as more of a solicitor, a vendor, or a peer to your upstream referral partners?

___

How can you start to transition your identity in your own eyes, in the eyes of your customers and prospective customers, and in the eyes of your upstream partners to that of being a valuable peer?

___

Who is an upstream partner for your upstream partner?

___

6

FROM VENDOR TO PEER TO MENTOR AND LEADER

Often the knee-jerk reaction of others based solely on the job title on your business card is that you are a solicitor, someone motivated by trying to solve your own problem of not having enough business.

As you follow the model, a couple of things will happen. The first will be that you will start to get referrals to the clients of your upstream partners. The second thing that will happen is that you will shift from being just another vendor to being a peer to the upstream partner. You won't be seen as someone coming to "get value," but someone able and desirous to "give value."

In Chapter 5 we learned how to find upstream partners, how to connect with them, and how to create a value proposition that integrates us into conversations that these partners have on a regular basis with *their* clients.

We're now ready to advance this identity shift beyond just being a peer to that of being a mentor and leader. In so doing, you will be able to offer value to your upstream partners like never before.

```
                    ┌─────────────┐
                    │ MENTOR AND  │   RECOGNIZED AS AND LOOKED UP TO
                    │   LEADER    │   AS AN EXPERT, AN ADVISOR, A CON-
                    └─────────────┘   SULTANT, AND A LEADER: SOMEONE
                           ⇧          WHO CAN HELP SOLVE THE UPSTREAM
                                      PARTNER'S BIGGEST CHALLENGES
┌──────────┐        ┌─────────────┐
│ UPSTREAM │        │    PEER     │   LOOKED AT WITH RESPECT AS AN
│ PARTNER  │        │             │   EQUAL IN A DIFFERENT INDUSTRY
└──────────┘        └─────────────┘
                           ⇧
                    ┌─────────────┐   HAS A SALES RELATIONSHIP WITH THE
                    │   VENDOR    │   UPSTREAM PARTNER, BUT
                    │             │   NOT SEEN AS AN EQUAL
                    └─────────────┘
                           ⇧
                    ┌─────────────┐
                    │  SOLICITOR  │   LOOKED UPON AS SOMEONE THERE TO
                    │             │   GET SOMETHING FOR THEMSELVES
                    └─────────────┘
```

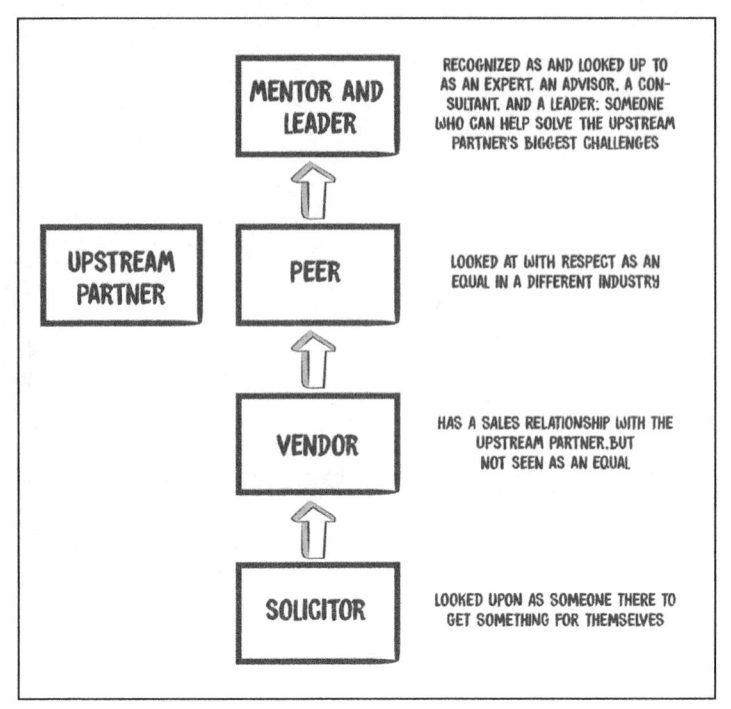

FIGURE 4: UPSTREAM MODEL IDENTITY PROGRESSION

IF YOU WANT MY BUSINESS, BECOME A PART OF MY BUSINESS

One of my first big meetings that I got as a title sales executive with a top real estate agent was one that I'll never forget. Nick already had a solid relationship in place that took great care of his title and escrow needs. Meanwhile, he had also grown unaccustomed to sales executives from different title companies approaching him as solicitors or vendors to try to capture his attention and loyalties. Similar to how my stepmom described these attempts, they weren't helpful enough for him to change his loyalties. The only reasons that he took the meeting with me were because

- I was introduced to Nick through a mortgage loan officer that Nick respected, and
- I was genuinely interested in the topic of a book that Nick was finishing at the time.

During our first meeting, Nick quickly cut to the chase and gave me the same challenge that he gave all of my competitors who came to meet with him: *Help me to promote my book.*

Like a lovely slow-pitch softball lob over home plate, Nick told me exactly what he wanted me to do to get his attention. Like my competitors, at first, I thought small. I immediately thought about a few individual agents with whom I could share his book. Fortunately for me, before I left that meeting, Nick made a comment that stuck with me. He quoted a well-known author and sales trainer who had said *"If you want someone's business, you need to become a part of their business."*

For the rest of that day, this quote ran through my mind what felt like a hundred times. I wanted Nick's business, for sure, and he just gave me the recipe for what I needed to do to get it. I thought, *If I were a part of Nick's business, would I just tell a few people about his book, or would I take it to a whole new level?*

You already know the answer.

Within a few days I had made a list of many of the major real estate podcasts around the country. If I was going to be valuable to Nick, I needed to strategically add to my network. I began letting these podcast hosts know about Nick's upcoming book and the major problem that it solved. I also informed them that Nick had a media background and would be an excellent interview for their shows. The bookings started to take place and Nick was impressed. Keep in mind that, before this, I had no idea how to promote a book. Yet I wanted Nick's business badly enough that I figured it out.

By uncovering a real concern, and devoting attention and energy around solving the problem, I moved myself out of the role of solicitor and vendor into being one of Nick's peers. He now respected me and saw me more as a partner in helping him to reach his goals. I even began to learn and gain expertise on additional ways to promote and monetize the sale of a book. This moved me out of the role of peer into now being able to mentor and lead Nick in things that he needed to know. From this experience, Nick and I built a friendship, and it was not long before he was referring his clients to our company.

One of the regular concerns that comes up is *Who am I to be mentoring my upstream partners?*

One of my personal mentors, Russell Brunson, spoke about how to overcome this in his book *Expert Secrets* when he referenced the box-office hit *Catch Me If You Can*. In the movie, Leonardo DiCaprio plays the part of a sophisticated con artist who pretended to be everything from an airplane pilot, to a doctor, to a university professor. When asked how one pulls off being a university professor, he shared that he didn't need to know everything about that particular course of study; he just needed to be one chapter ahead of his students. While neither my mentor or I recommend that you become a con artist by any means, most of us mistakenly think that to become a mentor, we must know more than those we are mentoring in *all areas*. In contrast, the reality is that a mentor needs only to know more than their mentees in *one area*.

Choosing to gain expertise in something that solves a problem for your upstream partner that they have not already solved is key. Unique to Nick's situation was that, even before the first meeting, I knew the source of Nick's biggest challenge. While it isn't always that simple, it's also not as hard as we often make it out to be. Sometimes it is as simple as asking your upstream partners or others close to them, while at other times you may need an alternative strategy.

One strategy that I've employed for years is helping my upstream partners with a fourth quarter business planning session. With the combined help of some tremendous mentors, I've developed what I believe to be one of the better business planning templates and workshops in the real estate industry. I openly offer to help my upstream partners to create their business plan through a sixty minute workshop, and I do this for a couple of distinct reasons.

First, through this process, I get to position myself as a peer and even a mentor as we walk through that process together. Secondly, I gain unbelievable intelligence on where they are at now and where they want to be at 1 year, 5 years, and 10 years from now. We cover the "why" behind these goals, the "what" their business needs to achieve in order to hit those goals, and the "how" of actually making that a reality.

By retaining a copy of their plan, I am able to make contact with these upstream partners quarterly to check in to see if they are "on plan." Through these pre-scheduled reviews, we are able to celebrate the wins while also discussing what changes they need to make to get back on track in hitting their one-year goals. This allows me to identify additional ways that I can be of value and a part of their business moving forward.

Another powerful strategy is an upstream mastermind.

Masterminds Aren't Worth My Time

"Hey Marc, this is Justin. Steve told me to call you. He spoke so highly of you, mentioned that we have a lot in common, and told me that we definitely need to meet."

"Hey, Justin," Marc replied.

Marc was a top real estate agent, and I was calling as a title sales executive.

He continued, "I appreciate Steve wanting us to sit down, but I'm really committed to my existing title company, even to the point that our families vacation together. I just don't want to waste your time."

Of course, this was disappointing. But before ending the call, I made one last attempt to get some time with Marc. I resorted to an invitation where I wasn't the value offering—his peers were. I told him, "Would you be willing to come to a mastermind?"

The term "mastermind" was coined by Napoleon Hill, who in his broadcasts and books, including the classics *Think & Grow Rich*, *The Law of Success*, and *The Master Key to Riches*, taught the following:

> A mastermind alliance, now what many call a "mastermind group" is "a friendly alliance with one or more persons who will encourage one to follow through with both plan and purpose … It is the principle through which you can accomplish in one year more than you could accomplish without it in a lifetime if you depended entirely on your own efforts for success.

Sounds pretty amazing, right? So why in the world would Marc not be willing to attend one of these? Marc's response surprised me. He said,

"You know, I appreciate the invite, but I'm not a big fan of masterminds. I haven't always found them worth my time."

I thought, *Okay, this isn't going well.* But despite his answers, Marc's tone wasn't curt or rude, so I continued, "I'd love to hear what you don't like about masterminds."

Marc responded by telling me that he never knew either who was going to attend or the topic that was going to be covered. He wanted to know the who and the what of the mastermind in advance of committing to attend. This foreknowledge gave him a clue as to whether he'd see a positive return on his time invested, and I didn't fault him for that.

In the past, I had been a part of mastermind groups that had proven valuable for my businesses. Similarly, I believed that they would be a powerful way for me to deliver value to my upstream referral partners. Through a mastermind, I would be able to gather essential information that would reveal the biggest challenges and problems of my upstream referral partners.

Yet, if Marc had this concern and was unwilling to come, I knew others would feel that way as well. The way it stood, my credibility and my ability to offer value that mattered to Marc and others like him were fading.

Upstream Model Masterminds

After my conversation with Marc, I had to remind myself that for those of us eager to learn and grow, there is no failure; there is only feedback. With the help and mentorship of my friend and productivity coach, Jay Puppo, together with other top business minds, I sought and created a breakthrough. With these new ideas, I would be able to create a format that would overcome concerns that Marc had shared.

This format promoted more consistency in who attended, as well as more engagement since the attendees themselves became the source of the mastermind's topics. Over time I've refined this format, and it now fits perfectly into the broader framework of the Upstream Model. The following are the vital elements for it to be a success for everyone involved.

Mindset

Even before deciding who you want to invite, you must be very intentional that all those invited have a specific experience from the very outset. That experience ties into a fundamental principle that we learned previously: you are doing this to give, not to get. You are not there, nor is anyone there, to sell. It's not about promoting your brand, the unique features of your product or services, or anything similar. The moment you do that, you kill the mastermind, and people like Marc don't return. That mentality picks you up and drops you right back into the role of being a vendor.

Instead, you must get your head around the fact that you are there as a peer. For me, in the title and escrow industry, it was never about bringing in my title and escrow officers, or even about my leadership team. My attendance was as a *peer* to upstream partners. Those invited are top producers in their industry, and I'm a top producer in my industry. As a result, we have similar goals, ambitions, and concerns. We are not there to talk about how what I do for a profession can solve their problems. Instead, we are there to discuss how our combined experiences in business can help each of us take our respective companies to the next level.

You have to think of it as a board of directors meeting for everyone in attendance. Small businessowners, entrepreneurs, and intrapreneurs don't have the luxury of having their own board of directors, and so this is designed to be precisely that.

It cannot feel like any one company is putting this on to promote their brand. Again, that's what vendors do. If you want to keep thinking and acting that way, you'll continue to compete along a crowded shoreline for years to come, fighting for your very livelihood while tech firms work to squeeze you out of the picture altogether.

You may be thinking, *How am I supposed to lead a mastermind of my upstream partners when I've never run a legal practice, a financial advisory company, etc.?*

It's a great question. As a title sales executive, I was not, nor had I ever been, a licensed real estate agent. I did not have expertise in the profession of helping clients to buy and sell real estate. How did I navigate that?

1. I didn't profess to know something that I didn't know. I leaned on others in the group to answer operations-specific questions.

2. As I contributed during the event, I focused on topics that were common among all business professionals. These conversations allowed me to be relevant and valuable in the mastermind, further positioning me as a peer to the others in attendance.

There's an important principle embedded here. Regardless of your industry, business is business. Once we rise above the fray of the day-to-day in our respective companies, professionals have much in common. Although you may know very little to nothing about the daily comings and goings of your upstream partners' businesses and industries, the reality is that those in attendance spend the majority of their time working in their business. Under your leadership, they are not attending to discuss the work *in their business*. When done correctly, the attendees have set aside this time to be able to work *on their business*.

If done right, this will be the focus of the mastermind. In so doing, you will find yourself just as relevant and valuable to those outside your industry as you are to those in your industry.

Logistics

All invitees must see this mastermind as a very different proposition than a typical class, forum, roundtable, or luncheon that they've experienced in the past. They must recognize the difference themselves. The venue to which we are inviting our guests must reinforce this point. It must be different from those venues where they've attended any of these "typical" events. For example, a nice restaurant or country club would be appropriate. However, be sure to make it sustainable and accessible for those attending. And be creative! During the pandemic-related, when social distancing recommendations and precautions meant not being able to meet in person but rather than having another Zoom meeting, we had a catered lunch delivered to every attendee's home. In short, it had to look and feel different, i.e., better, exclusive, and special. Doing this also ensured attendees took the time to attend, provided their undivided attention throughout, and came in with a different mindset than they would if they were just popping into a continuing education class.

We also take special care to see to it that the invitations also look, feel, and sound different than anything they've experienced. Rather than an email with a link to sign up, the invitations that we put together look and feel more like a wedding announcement. They are a formal invitation on beautiful cardstock that mentions no sponsor (although for convenience with electronic schedules, we add a sign-up link). Our attendees' first exposure to the event was the formal invitation that felt more like that of a black-tie affair instead of a run-of-the-mill networking session.

Regarding frequency, monthly was too frequent, and semi-annually was too infrequent. Quarterly was the right choice. It gives those in attendance time to implement what they learned and to anticipate the next event.

Attendees

Who you invite into the mastermind is paramount. Attendance is not for just anyone. Additionally, being invited once doesn't mean you are automatically invited back. You must earn your way into this mastermind and continue earning your spot in the mastermind each time.

You might be thinking that if your upstream partners have the same concerns as Marc had about masterminds not being worth their time, how do you get them to come to that first one? It's as simple as getting the commitment from a couple of people who have a recognizable name or reputation and then leveraging those commitments to get the rest. Once they experience the event, you'll never have trouble getting them to come back.

When it comes to the criteria by which you choose your potential attendees, a few things are non-negotiables. Your invitees must be

- Upstream partners or potential upstream partners. I've found having a balance of current partners versus prospective partners allows those that are not already taking advantage of your value to hear about it from those that are.

- Ethical. We have to have a room of trustworthy people whose reputations precede them for other top producers and high caliber people to come and to return.

- High producers. Top producers will see right through a room of pretenders. Holding the line on this allows everyone to receive and give value during the event. If someone isn't at that level, they may observe and receive a lot of value, yet they likely won't be emitting much in return. Others in the room feel this, and it lessens the experience for all. Or, worse, a lower producer speaks up to ask for help on a minor league problem that isn't valuable to others in the group.

- Likeminded. All in attendance need to have, in a general sense, a standard set of concerns, challenges, and problems as a result of having a business that is similar in size to others in the room. These similarities allow the mastermind to be relevant and a synergistic experience for all.

- Growth minded. When people come hungry to learn, learning happens.

- Generous. Insecurity invites ego. When you have someone who is a producer and is humble and generous with expertise, all benefit.

Mastermind Meeting Start

Attendees are greeted and then given a chance to mingle with and get caught up with their mastermind peers for a few minutes. The energy from this is always a great way to start. Shortly after that, we sit and get down to business. We then start by laying some ground rules for all to follow. Of course, with the caliber of attendees, there is no strict need to say any of the rules, but we do so anyway so that everyone is clear. I restate them every time:

Ethics. You are hand-selected to be a part of this mastermind event because of your reputation and your integrity. We encourage you to take everything you learn here and apply it. What will not be tolerated, of course, is to take something that you learn about one of your fellow mastermind partners and use it to hurt them.

Respect. We have limited time, and so we ask that no one person dominates the conversation. Please allow and encourage others to speak up.

Follow-up. In the two hours that we spend together, we won't possibly extract all the value available. We welcome and invite you to follow up with your peers afterward to provide and ask for help and mentorship.

Intention. I'm here as a peer from a different industry. I intend to help each of us to identify and then solve our respective businesses' most significant concerns and challenges.

Customized Value for Everyone

While considering what Marc had said about the risk of attending a mastermind whose topic was not relevant to his concerns, I discovered something interesting. According to Napoleon Hill's definition of a mastermind, Marc had not been attending masterminds. He had been attending classes disguised as masterminds.

The purpose of a true mastermind is to solve the concerns of each of those in the group. The upstream format includes the following two general topic categories, which allow this to happen.

1. **What is working.** After we lay the ground rules and run quickly through introductions, we begin with the first exercise, which allows all to share what is working well in their respective businesses. For the sake of time, we do not give people time to expound. If anyone hears something that intrigues them during this segment, I invite them to connect with that participant after the meeting.

2. **Biggest challenge.** Each participant gets a chance to share what their biggest challenge is briefly. As a board of directors

would, we work through and offer solutions and ideas to help that person solve that particular problem. We then move on to the next person. This exercise allows us to get the collective wisdom of everyone in the group, solving each attendees' current biggest concern and challenge. Put similarly, quoting the focusing question from the book *The ONE Thing* by Gary Keller and Jay Papasan: *What is the one thing you could do such that by doing it would make everything else easier or unnecessary?*

Occasionally, I'll remind those in attendance to look around the room and consider the collective experience and wisdom that they have at their very fingertips. Not only does this cause them to take seriously the opportunity to solve significant problems but it is also a vivid reminder of the value that they are receiving by being in my inner circle of upstream referral partners.

I always prefer having an administrative assistant in the room to take copious notes so that the attendees can focus on what they do best (thinking and talking and sharing) instead of having to take their own notes. The added benefit of this is that, at the end of the meeting, I have a nicely summarized value-add gift to offer all those that attended.

Keep in mind that my intent is recognition from my upstream partner peers that I am more than another vendor and that I am not there just to host the meeting. I do not talk about my specific company offerings but participate in the mastermind, helping to solve my peers' most significant concerns. Doing this gives me another opportunity to demonstrate myself in the role of a valued expert, consultant, advisor, and leader. Imagine the paradigm shift they're having, not just about me as a peer but me as a referral partner, someone with whom they could entrust their very client referrals.

Mastermind Wrap-up and Follow-up

As our time expires, I thank everyone for their participation. I reinforce the value I received: I walk away with a detailed list of the biggest concerns of my upstream referral partners together with the collective advice and wisdom of a room full of top-producing peers regarding how they would go about solving those very problems. It's pure gold! This comment implies that they also received a similar benefit from attending the mastermind. I let them know that the notes will be shared in the coming days once we have a chance to clean them up.

Concerning the follow-up, imagine how much easier it would be to bring value to those who attended. It's like shooting fish in a barrel. I know their most significant challenge, together with the suggested solutions from the collective wisdom of their respected and trusted peers. You can, therefore, imagine how much easier a phone call to Marc would be now. My follow-up call looks like this:

Hey Marc, it's Justin. I wanted to take a quick second and thank you for attending our mastermind. It was great having you there. I also wanted to let you know that I've been thinking about what you shared as your biggest concern. I loved what a few of the other attendees suggested as ways to solve those concerns, and I wanted to see if we could schedule a few minutes to discuss how I can help you implement those ideas. Would you be open to that?

Yes, those invitations to meet on that premise are almost always accepted. I'm coming into the conversation knowing what Marc's biggest challenge is. Additionally, I go in armed with the solutions suggested by his most respected peers. I'm now offering my time and expertise to be sure those ideas get implemented, and this challenge gets put to rest. That's a powerful place to be.

The reality is that Marc initially declined because he had not been attending masterminds. He had been attending classes disguised as masterminds about topics that may not have been relevant and with people who may not have been peers and potential mentors. Now, compare that with what Marc just experienced. Very different, right?

Here's what Marc said, which is similar to what almost everyone says: "Justin, I can't thank you enough for inviting me. I loved my time there, and I hope I get invited back. I'd love to get together to discuss further. What works well for you?"

In summary, to those upstream partners who can massively impact the number of referrals that I have coming into my business, my identity has changed. In the mastermind, I became a peer. By following up after the mastermind to help solve the problems shared, I become a mentor and a leader, someone to whom Marc looks to help solve his most significant challenges.

In the following chapter, we're going to discuss how the most valuable companies in the world are data companies. I'll then give you a different way to think about your own business and value proposition that will allow you to position yourself with a similar mindset and strategy, thereby significantly upgrading the value that you bring to the marketplace.

ASSERTIONS

- *If you want someone's business, you need to become a part of their business.*

- *Masterminds, when done right, can be powerful tools for gaining the intelligence needed to bring very customized help to your upstream partners' most significant challenges and problems.*

- *When done correctly, masterminds allow you to go from being a vendor to being a peer.*

- *When done correctly, the follow-up after a mastermind allows you to go from being a peer to a mentor and a leader.*

REFLECTIONS

Who are critical upstream referral partners that you would like to have at a mastermind event?

_____

Who are the two or three people you could invite whose names and reputations would help fill the room?

_____

Where could you host this mastermind that doesn't break the budget, yet would allow those attending to feel a part of something different, better, unique, and more exclusive than just another class?

_____

How quickly would you be able to host your first mastermind?

_____

7

YOUR DATA Base

One of the critical lessons shared in Chapter 6 is the importance of the data and insights extracted from an upstream mastermind. Remember, with relation to your upstream partners, the desired outcome of the mastermind is to do two things.

First, continue to shift your identity from a solicitor/vendor to their peer. Solicitors and vendors show up with their hand out, looking for referrals without thought of offering value beyond what they do for a living. They are very focused on what's in it for them in the short term. As a peer, however, you are an equal who can add value and/or solve similar problems and challenges that exist in your own business and the upstream partner's business. You are looking to add value without the need for immediate reciprocation.

Upstream mastermind events give you the ability to come together with your upstream partners to build relationships and to demonstrate that *you want* to help offer solutions to their problems and that *you can* provide solutions to their problems. Also, the help that you provide extends beyond the confines of what you do for a living.

Second, gather data and insights around the biggest challenges faced by your upstream referral partners so that you can begin shifting to being their mentor and leader. Additionally, helping your upstream partners apply the combined wisdom of all those in attendance becomes an extension of your offering, your mentorship, and your leadership.

The next phase of understanding and living the Upstream Model is the understanding that you must pivot the way that you now think about and position your business to imitate the most valuable companies in the world.

THE IDENTITY & BUSINESS MODEL SHIFT

"We are no longer a coaching and training company that sells real estate. We are now pivoting to become a technology company."

February 2018, I sat in the Anaheim Convention Center and listened to Gary Keller, cofounder and CEO of Keller Williams Realty (KW), the largest real estate franchise in the world by agent count, make this startling announcement. Just previously, KW was voted by *Training Magazine* as the number-one training organization across all industries worldwide. With this in mind, you can imagine how pivoting from being known as a training company to being a technology company surprised everyone.

Keller justified his bold move by highlighting how many of the highest-valued companies in the world were once natural resource companies, like oil and gas. Then, only 10 years later, those top spots were mostly occupied by companies based on the technology platform model. See image below.

Largest Global Companies in 2018 vs 2008:
In 2018, seven out of ten were based on the platform model

\-	2018	\-	\-	\-	2008	\-	\-
RANK	COMPANY	FOUNDED	USBn	RANK	COMPANY	FOUNDED	USBn
1	Apple*	1976	890	1	PetroChina	1999	728
2	Google*	1998	768	2	Exxon	1870	492
3	Microsoft*	1975	680	3	General Electric	1892	358
4	Amazon*	1994	592	4	China Mobile	1997	344
5	Facebook*	2004	545	5	ICBC	1984	336
6	Tencent*	1998	526	6	Gazprom	1989	332
7	Berkshire Hathaway	1955	496	7	Microsoft	1975	313
8	Alibaba.com*	1999	483	8	Shell	1907	266
9	Johnson & Johnson	1886	380	9	Sinopec (China)	2000	257
10	J.P.Morgan	1871	375	10	AT&T	1885	238

*Companies based on the platform model

Source: Bloomberg, Google

FIGURE 5: DIGITAL COMPANY

What are technology platform companies and why are they the most valuable in the world? A technology platform company is one that involves not only one company's service or technology but also an ecosystem of complementary offers that are most often produced by a variety of businesses. Maybe your mind has gone to the complementary offers that we've been discussing when you align with the right upstream partners.

While direct revenue is one reason these companies are so valuable, another is what some may consider the real gold mine. Technology companies are highly valuable because they can turn the analyzed data of millions of users into highly coveted customer insights. While data is defined as the information gathered, insights are what that data tells us about what consumers will want, need, or do next. These insights act as a crystal ball for the company collecting the data and for other companies to whom they can sell these insights.

A prime example of this in the real estate industry is Zillow. Zillow has built a real estate platform that millions of consumers prefer. The data they collect allows them to come up with insights around who wants to buy, who wants to sell, who wants to refinance their mortgage, etc. Zillow can sell those insights back to the real estate industry in the form of customer leads. In addition to selling these insights, Zillow is also now capitalizing directly on these data insights by becoming a brokerage with their own agents who will now compete directly with what used to be their customers. Additionally, at the time of this writing, they also have their Zillow Offers program in which there is no agent involved. Instead, Zillow purchases the home directly from the seller.

By focusing on getting customers on their platforms, gathering customers' data, and creating insights that they and others can act on, massive technology portals like Zillow and Redfin have company valuations in the multiple billions. These valuations surpass the estimated value of every other traditional real estate company on the planet.

Gary Keller's pivot was motivated by this fact: unless his company acted fast to regain the hearts and minds of consumers by building the technology that they prefer and controlling the data collected, the outcome for their traditional agents would not be good. That "undesirable outcome" for real estate agents would be to become low-paid functionaries working for big tech, rather than well-paid fiduciaries empowered by tech.

At the time of writing this book, the verdict is still out as to if KW can build technology that agents and consumers prefer. Critics argue that it is too little too late and that they are ill-equipped to compete against these tech giants. Meanwhile, others say that KW's efforts and other people-centric, tech-focused brokerages like eXp Realty, a cloud-based brokerage model, are now taking the oxygen out of the space where these big tech disruptors once thrived.

Regardless of their fate, the bold moves by these companies should be a clarion call and lesson to all people-centric, service-based industries that

1. we, too, must get and keep the attention of our customers, potential customers, and upstream partners by offering the service and value they prefer; and

2. as we serve these customers and upstream partners, we should intentionally gather data that we can formulate into insights as to how we can best serve them, and others like them.

Now, please don't misinterpret what I'm saying. I am not saying that you should trade out your business of servicing customers for writing code to become a technology platform company.

Here's what I am saying: If you want to remain relevant and valuable in the marketplace moving forward, it would be wise to follow the lead of the most valuable companies in the world and recognize that the complementary offers that you have, the data that you collect, and the insights that you derive from this data are paramount in keeping and retaining the attention and business of your current and future customers and upstream partners.

HEY CHARLIE MUNGER, HERE'S A QUESTION FOR YOU

Each year at the largest spectator arena in Omaha, Nebraska, over 18,000 shareholders gather from all over the world to get an update on one of the most successful investment holding companies of all time, Berkshire Hathaway. As interested as they are in an update on the company's financial holdings, it is safe to say that those that attend are just as interested in learning directly from legendary investors, Warren Buffett, the company's Chairman and CEO, and Charlie Munger, the company's Vice Chairman.

At one point, an attendee asked the following question to Charlie: "What was the most valuable investment that you ever made?"

You can imagine the anticipation of the crowd in hearing this legendary investor's answer. Naturally, each of the event's attendees likely anticipated hearing him speak of an investment made in some formerly unknown company, which then became a successful household name or brand. Instead, Charlie's response surprised people when he pointed to a more obscure incident. He had approved spending several hundred thousand dollars to a headhunter recruiting company that helped them to find a CEO for one of the businesses they owned. This CEO, tasked with turning the business around, did just that. That six-digit investment created a return better than any other investment he has made.

This a powerful takeaway for you and me. The most valuable investment made by one of the world's greatest investor minds of all time, the vice chairman of possibly the most significant investment holding company of all time, wasn't that of buying or investing in a company in the traditional sense. Instead, it was an investment to find the right person, the right leader, who then changed everything for one of their companies.

If the lesson isn't yet obvious, here's another way to look at it. Do you know a lot of people? Have you ever made an introduction from one person to another that was valuable to both parties? Do you think that, if you were even a bit more intentional than you have been in the past, you could do more of that? My strong assumption is that you answered yes to each of those questions.

If the best investment that Charlie Munger ever made was in getting an introduction to the right person, consider this: how capable are you of taking the data and insights that you have about people in your database and leveraging it to make introductions that bring value, potentially career-changing or even life-changing value, to others?

THE POWER OF YOUR DATABASE

The Upstream Model has given us the blueprint for getting more referrals from fewer relationships by leveraging uncommon thinking, strategies, and tactics with upstream partners. Recognizing the power of data and insights accelerates your ability to bring value to these partners and the customers that they refer.

Think for just a minute about the number of people and the amount of data that you have access to as you go about doing what you do. Let's take a real estate agent, for example. You have clients as well as prospective clients' names, phone numbers, addresses, spouses' names, contact info, family member names, job information, motives for living where they live, and how much they're pre-approved to spend on a home.

Additionally, if you're intentional, relational, and wise, you will also know birthdays, wedding anniversaries, home purchase anniversaries, favorite restaurants, and preferred hobbies, recreation, and vacation spots. You may know the challenges they have had, do have, or anticipate having. You may learn of their goals and dreams of what they want life to look like in the future.

As a financial advisor or a mortgage loan officer, you not only know many of the things that a real estate agent knows, but you know more detailed information about your customer's financial life. Using the well-known SWOT analysis acronym, concerning their financial life, you know their strengths, weaknesses, opportunities, and threats.

As you are intentional about the data that you collect, and the insights you derive from that data, those insights can become beneficial to the upstream partners you serve. You'll be able to help them better serve their clients, retain their databases, and get more referrals from their upstream referral partners.

Database Redefined

When people hear the word database, they often think solely of their client relationship management (CRM) tool. While having an accurate, regularly updated CRM is critical for you to leverage all that you know to systematically and consistently add value to your customers and upstream partners, there's more to it than this electronic filing system that holds customer data.

One of my mentors defined a database as a list of relationships. While that does the job of differentiating a database from a mailing list, in a day and age of data-driven companies, this definition now falls short. One way to define database could be to include

- Who you know
- Who you *could* know
- What you know
- What you *could* know

Who You Know

Consider for a moment how many contacts you have in your database. Regardless of whether you have them all neatly organized, think about combining the relationships you have in your CRM software with other places you have lists of relationships. For example, your phone, your email contacts, and your social media accounts like LinkedIn, Facebook, and others. Consider all the relationships in this combined list to be included in your definition of a database. I suspect that this combined number of contacts is likely in the hundreds, if not thousands of people.

To reinforce what I shared above, I want to invite you to think about the opportunities to add value that would arise if you were intentional at identifying the biggest challenges of your upstream partners. Now, consider the possibility of making an introduction between someone in your database, or even your database's database, and an upstream partner that solves their "biggest challenge." What kind of value could you bring into their business and even into their life? Could you make one introduction that, looking back, made all the difference in your company?

My experience has been that, without remarkable effort, I have been able to offer introductions that make a notable difference for my upstream partners. I'm confident that the same is true for you.

Who You Could Know

The value that we can deliver today is not the same as the value that we can deliver tomorrow. That is in part because the network of people we know today is not as powerful as the network of people that we can know tomorrow. When we choose to invest in upstream partner relationships, we start to think and act differently with regard to the people we don't yet know but could know.

In my day-to-day work with real estate agents, I created the following conversation to help them intentionally grow their network with other professionals, making them more valuable to their customers and their upstream partners.

> *As a real estate agent, I have the good fortune of meeting a lot of people. I make it a point to learn as much as I can, both personally and professionally, about those whom I meet. This information allows me to be more valuable than just having expertise in marketing and selling properties. My clients get access not only to my real estate skill set, they also get access to my network of people and professionals who can help to solve their problems or open new doors of opportunity. I'd love to meet with you, learn more about you, and see if there are some ways that my client base and referral partners may benefit by knowing you and your business.*

This conversation does three things:

1. Attracts professionals into your database who also serve their clients at the highest levels.

2. Educates the professional that you are looking to add value to people and professionals, not just get another property sale.

3. Reinforces that your value proposition as a real estate agent is different than just helping people buy and sell real estate. It teaches and strengthens the point that when clients work with you, and when upstream partners align with you, they get someone in their corner whose database and value proposition is always growing.

What You Already Know

Unless you are a teenager, you know more than you think you do. If you were to take the summation of your formal and informal education, couple it with your myriad of life experiences, lessons, and principles learned, what you derive would fill a book. This summation would likely even fill volumes of books. If you're not yet convinced, here's a story to illustrate.

When I was 19 years old, I served a two-year mission for my church. I didn't get to choose where I went, yet I don't think I could have dreamed of a better place to be assigned. I served in the Rio de Janeiro North Mission. The southern end of our mission area was the city of Rio de Janeiro. Our mission boundary extended north up the coast the distance of about a 10-hour car ride into the neighboring Brazilian state named Espirito Santo.

For two years, I kept a journal in which I wrote a little about my experiences each day, and more importantly, what I learned that day. My daily entries were not long, and each physical journal was about 100 pages long. In just two years, merely documenting my experiences, I filled five of those journals. Yes, in just two years, I filled five large-page, small-font journal books that logged my experiences and education.

Just recently, I've revived this practice of journaling. I make an entry each day in our family journal and another short entry in a personal journal. Although I'm excited to one day share this with my children, the point that I want to make is that if we are intentional, each one of us could also fill page after page after page of life experiences, lessons, and principles learned, and we could do it faster than we think. Whether or not we formalize all of this into an actual journal, every one of us has a private database of knowledge and wisdom from which we can create insights to mentor and lead those we serve.

What You Could Know

Your reading of this book tells me that you are an ambitious professional, hungry to learn and grow. By directing your attention and focusing your learning on solving the most significant problems and challenges faced by your upstream partners, you can prove to be of tremendous value to your upstream partners and the customers that they refer.

Once I discover what the challenges of my upstream partners are, I make it a point to go online to search for the book most likely to help solve my upstream partners' most significant concerns. I then send them a picture of the cover to let them know what I'm reading and then extend the offer to connect for a few minutes in the coming month to share what I have learned and how it may be of benefit to solving their challenge.

In this way, you are not only willing to share who you know and what you know to solve their problem. You're now also suggesting that an affiliation with you means that your upstream partner is going to get access to everything you *could know*.

While giving a book as a gift causes you to stand out, the knowledge you've offered them, without the typical expenditure of time to acquire that knowledge, has made you extremely different and extremely valuable. You've brought insights into your value proposition that can serve your upstream referral partner effectively and powerfully. Additionally, the knowledge that you gained by learning how to solve that particular challenge is now yours and can be used with other upstream partners as well. This example is one way to get your pole in the water and fish on the line along a very crowded shoreline.

Keep in mind that this is just one tactic. You do not have to go around reading books to add value to your upstream partners. Some might even argue that this may not be feasible, that it may be unnecessary, or even over the top. A quick Google search followed by a 10-minute YouTube video from an expert in this area may be more than enough to solve the challenge and prove your willingness and ability to solve their problem. While Google is at everyone's fingertips, not everyone takes the time and initiative to leverage it to this level. Doing it for a partner is beyond uncommon and causes you to really stand out.

THE GOLD MINES AND OIL WELLS OF TODAY

Years ago, the most valuable resources on earth were found in gold mines, diamond mines, and oil wells. Now, living in the information age and with the rise of big tech that grabs, stores, and mines data, we must pivot the way that we think about our businesses. We don't need to build a technology platform; however, by recognizing the tremendous amounts of data to which we have access and mining it for insights to help our upstream partners and the customers that they refer to us, the more wealth we'll uncover for ourselves.

Each of us can begin to model powerful data companies by intentionally growing our database of who we know, who we could know, what we know, and what we could know. Then, by deliberately sharing those insights with our upstream partners to solve their biggest challenges, the time, energy, and resources that they invest in us may end up being the best investment they ever make. In so doing, our businesses begin to follow the lead of the world's most valuable companies.

Thus far, we've learned how to get more referrals from fewer relationships. For those who have even bigger ambitions. For those who want to take the principles we've learned and scale them to serve more people at this higher level, the next chapter is for you.

ASSERTIONS

- *Data companies are now the most valuable companies in the world.*

- *As you pivot to think and act like a data company, you'll be increasing your value proposition, improving your margins, and insulating yourself against industry disruption.*

- *Who and what you know now, coupled with who and what you could know in the future, make your value proposition invincible, out of reach of industry disruption and the common professional.*

REFLECTIONS

What system or tools do you currently use (CRM or other) to store data and insights that you're gaining from your database?

———————————————————————————

What questions could you start asking your clients and upstream partners that would help you to begin adding valuable relationships and insights into that database?

———————————————————————————

What is a book you could read, a podcast that you could listen to, or a mentor whose videos you could watch that would allow you to offer valuable help to an upstream referral partner?

———————————————————————————

8

EXTENDING YOUR REACH

In the previous chapter, we learned of an essential pivot in mindset and strategic positioning for our respective businesses that allows us to follow the path of the most valuable companies in the world. We learned, in a sense, to think and act like a technology platform company, yet on a more micro and personal level.

This paradigm shift gives us the ability to acquire, retain, and effectively use data to offer relevant, unique, and valuable insights to our clients and our upstream referral partners. Doing so allows us to become a more valuable part of their business, making getting their referrals natural and an obvious by-product.

Part of the magic of the Upstream Model is that you can offer such value to these upstream partners that they actively find referrals for you from within their client base. Additionally, because of the way that you are approaching and offering value to these partners, you enter into the lives of their customers edified as a mentor and leader as opposed to showing up as just another vendor.

Yet, if you're highly ambitious, you are going to need and want to continue to find additional ways to scale your efforts. This ambition requires that extending your reach must always be a priority.

BUDDING HOPE

"Steve, we just got our first order from the SellPDX team, and they said that more is on the way!"

I was driving along Meadows Road, a high-end business district in Lake Oswego, a suburb of Portland, Oregon, when I made that call. The tulips were coming up, the trees were starting to form their buds, and the excitement and anticipation for longer, dryer days were felt by all after a typical long, dark, and wet Portland winter.

I was hungry for spring. Not just for the season but also the spring of my career. I had closed my general contracting company at the bottom of the financial crisis, and then during the early years of the recovery, I had worked for companies and in roles that were not the right long-term fit. After what felt like a long winter, I was hopeful that the momentum I was gaining was the beginning of something new.

Although the crisis had passed and its resultant difficult circumstances were behind me, I still struggled with certain doubts and fears:

- Would the real estate industry fall hard again?

- Was working for a big company rather than building my own business a cop-out?

- How long could a job keep my attention before I got bored and wanted to be back into being in business for myself?

- Would I disappoint or let down those who took a chance on me and hired me?

- Could I get customers to leave their longstanding title and escrow relationships?

As Steve and I spoke and celebrated another win, my hope for what was possible continued to grow. We were both excited, and not just because of the new revenue that this would produce. We were excited because of what this and previous wins were telling us about what we had to offer.

Our upstream partners were choosing us over their previous relationships. They weren't doing it because they were dissatisfied with the level of service that they or their clients had been getting. Just the opposite. They were often leaving their previous providers despite personal friendships and excellent service. They were coming to us because we were solving even more significant problems than those we got paid to solve. They believed that their possibilities would expand by being in business with us.

Steve's next comment changed me and my focus. He said, "The biggest challenge you have is that not enough people know about you."

Steve's advice was consistent with the words of one of my mentors, Grant Cardone, who said, "It's not how many people you know, but how many people know you."

Both Steve and I realized that the strategies and tactics I had been employing were unique and had the potential to help us reach our operation's revenue growth goals while also challenging the status quo of an industry that needed innovators. The challenge in front of me now was how do I get in front of more people faster? How do I grow my business and my identity of being a mentor and a leader simultaneously and quickly?

SCALING YOUR BUSINESS & YOUR IDENTITY

It is not enough to be known by more potential upstream partners if the perception is that you are just another solicitor or vendor. From their first impression of you, you must instill confidence in their minds that not only are you offering something different and better but that *you are* different and better.

Even more important than that, they need to know that, by gaining access to you, they will be able to offer something different and better to *their* clients, and that in time, with your mentorship and leadership, they will become someone different and better. They have to believe that, by being in business with you, their possibilities expand.

However, there is a challenge when you seek to simultaneously grow your service-based business and your identity to mentor and leader. That challenge lies in the fact that, frequently, you are the value proposition. With only so much time and only so much of you to go around, you quickly find yourself, once again, tapped and capped.

By focusing on adding value to a few upstream partners rather than on hundreds of people you know as friends, family, former customers, or community members, you have already improved your chances of scaling your growth. Through the upstream mastermind strategy, with 8 to 12 upstream referral partners in the room at once, you have yet another way to magnify and scale those same efforts.

When done correctly, these strategies allow you to get more referrals from fewer relationships. However, the last and final step in converting customers and upstream partners is almost always some form of a one-on-one meeting, which can cause you to bump into another ceiling quickly. Granted, it is a higher ceiling than the one you hit using traditional warm and cold markets, but like me, you may have ambitions that extend even beyond this new ceiling.

The question then remains: how do you scale your business and your identity simultaneously?

From Meeting Host to Meeting Keynote

When we think of scaling, our minds often go from a one-to-one model to a one-to-many, where you, for example, would be in front of a room full of your upstream partners. My upstream masterminds caused me to further reflect on how else I might be able to be in front of more upstream referral partners at once. I uncovered another interesting observation.

There exists a stark difference in the pay of a meeting organizer versus that of a keynote speaker.

Here's why that matters. Service-based industries have limited models for offering value using a one-to-many approach. In the title and escrow industry, it is a common practice to organize continuing education classes and seminars for upstream partners.

Although our upstream partners openly appreciated the offering, this common practice involves the title sales executive taking on the identity of a meeting organizer, a party planner of sorts. In other words, they have little to no expertise in sharing valuable content with the audience. Nor do they have an awareness of the importance of creating an opportunity to do so. Their self-selected role is to bring the food, coordinate the logistics of the presenter, and then offer a quick elevator pitch on why everyone present should use their company's services. This approach is very "vendor-like," and in no way, shape, or form would upstream partners see that person as a peer, a mentor, or a leader.

With that in mind, I began to ask myself how much money a meeting organizer/party planner got paid. The reality is, not very much—right around minimum wage, maybe a little more.

The follow-up question upon which I reflected was *"How much money does a keynote speaker get paid?"* For a good speaker, around $5,000 per hour (minimum). Meanwhile, others with massive value and celebrity command upwards of $100,000 for that same hour-long keynote speech! From minimum wage to $100,000, what a difference! While I have dramatized the gap between the two, you get my point: the one mentoring and leading on stage is highly compensated. Meanwhile, those who are the vendors handling meeting logistics are not.

Naturally, I wanted to start moving out of the role of being a meeting organizer and into that of being a keynote speaker. Rather than spending all my time sourcing other speakers and presenters of classes and presentations, I began to spend time developing my content around solutions to my upstream partners' most significant challenges. As the creator and keynote, you are no longer there just to give an elevator sales pitch and then pass it over to the speaker who is there to offer the "real value." You are the real value, and your compensation follows.

So that you don't overthink this, the same lessons that we learned about being a mentor apply to being a keynote speaker. To be a successful keynote speaker, you don't have to know more than your audience in all areas. You just need to know more than the audience in some area. Simply start reallocating a little time each day to develop your expertise on topics that will matter when you present them to a room full of upstream partners as the keynote speaker.

The Opportunity of Video

As we continue learning how to scale our business and our identity simultaneously, we cannot ignore the opportunity that video presents.

As a title and escrow sales executive, the opportunity with video had become almost a necessity for the ambitious. For years and years, title sales executive competitors in my space requested meetings with enviable upstream partners. They then failed to deliver sufficient value during those meetings to make it a worthwhile investment of time. As a result of the stigma created over years and years of low-value meetings, even with utilizing the Upstream Model principles, getting that same face-to-face meeting opportunity with successful upstream partners was challenging.

While I was struggling to get these appointments, Facebook rolled out its Facebook Live feature. As they often do with new features, they were encouraging users to try it by giving significant favor in their algorithm to those that were crazy enough to stream live on their platform.

I was intrigued. I knew that the people with whom I wanted to be in business were often on Facebook and that I was either Facebook "friends" with them or that I could become "friends" with them without too much effort. I like to speak and teach, and so it didn't take me long to adopt this technology and begin getting comfortable with going live on Facebook. Within about a month, something interesting happened.

"Hey, Justin. I love your videos. They're really great..."

I began hearing those words regularly, including from upstream partners with whom I wanted to have a business relationship.

At one point, I had several people make a similar comment after my family and I had just returned from a several-day trip to an indoor water park called Great Wolf Lodge a few hours to the north. I recognized this powerful reality about a video that lives on a social media platform. While I was somewhere else, doing something else, my face, my voice, and my unique value proposition were mentoring and leading current and potential upstream partners.

I began to recognize that video was a fantastic source of leverage, and a secret doorway of sorts, into the offices and minds of those with whom I wanted to be in business the most. It also kept me top of mind and reinforced my unique value with those upstream partners with whom I already had a relationship. There were now no constraints on how many upstream partners I could be in front of, mentoring and leading them with my unique value.

This epiphany encouraged me to be even more consistent. I began shooting a live video almost every day of the week for several years in a row. *"Wait, did you say you shot a live video every day? Why so frequent? Isn't that kind of overkill?"* you might be asking. Allow me to explain my reasoning. If you take this to heart, it will hasten the pace at which you can scale your business and your identity.

One of my favorite mentors taught me the following principle. He said, "Don't overthink starting to create videos. Your first 100 videos are not for your audience anyway. Your first 100 videos are for you to figure out what you like to talk about. They are for you to find your voice."

As with anything, unless we repeatedly do it, we never get very good at it. Most people, when trying anything new, try it a few times, realize that they are bad at it, and then they never go back. What a losing formula.

In his classic book *Outliers*, Malcom Gladwell teaches that 10,000 is the magic number of times that one must do anything before achieving mastery. Although you do not need to attain mastery status before you see significant benefits from making videos, you also should not expect that you are going to be a movie star without putting in the work.

Fast forward to the time of writing this book, and I've now formalized my daily video into an episode of my show, the "Think Bigger Real Estate Show." As a result of my recorded interviews, I now get to learn from and share the stage, so to speak, with big thinking and high achieving influencers in business. These shows allow me to offer mentorship and leadership to my upstream partners at scale. My network, my knowledge, my business, and my identity as a mentor and a leader all grow simultaneously.

While working as the editor of *Success Magazine,* Darren Hardy once said, "I get to use the calling card of *Success Magazine* to be in conversation with some of the most successful people in the world." My strategy is similar. My show acts as that calling card for me, allowing me to spend time with the likes of Grant Cardone and others. I could never have convinced Grant and other big thinkers to spend time with me without the added leverage of sharing with them the platform I had been building for years. Figuring out the logistics, getting comfortable on camera, and finding my voice as the host of a show made that opportunity even a possibility. All of that took time, and all of that took being comfortable with not being good for an extended period prior. When I met Grant, I could not have invited him to be on a show that I did not yet have.

We have heard it said before that we must dig our well before we are thirsty. With video, this is true. We must acquire power and gain expertise before we need it. If we wait until we are good at it, we'll never start, and when the perfect opportunity comes along, we will not be positioned to take advantage of it.

The late Jim Rohn said, "You don't have to be great to start, but you do have to start to be great." Nothing could be more accurate about maximizing the limitless potential of using video to build your business and your identity.

My purpose in what I'm sharing here isn't to encourage you to do Facebook Live videos until you are ready to have your own show. That was my path. If that also speaks to you, great. I'll have resources and guides that can help you. What I am saying, however, is that we live in the most incredible time in the history of the world. When it comes to scaling, extending your reach, and getting your unique value proposition in front of an increasing number of upstream partners who can help you get more referrals from fewer relationships, do not underestimate the power of video.

JUST DO SOMETHING

Now, if the thought of video makes you want to stop reading, know that video is one method. Although I hope that you will reconsider, if that is not an option for you at this point and you prefer to be heard but not seen, start a podcast. If you prefer to have your ideas read but not heard or seen, then start a blog. The method of how you find and share your voice and your unique value proposition is not as crucial as just grabbing the mic, so to speak, and starting to share.

Since the time that my friend, mentor, and sales manager identified my most significant challenge that not enough people knew about me, things have changed. I am unable to attend any industry-related event without having someone approach me and thank me for the work that I do and the value that I offer through my show.

Now that we understand strategies for simultaneously scaling our business and our identity as a mentor and leader, in the next and final chapters, we are going to talk about the final step in our journey of understanding and living the Upstream Model. We are going to discuss the essential principle of leadership. Without this last piece, your efforts will be unsustainable and ineffective. Leadership is the keystone that holds together everything else we've discussed.

ASSERTIONS

- *Your biggest challenge is that not enough people know about you.*

- *The way to grow and scale is not just more one-to-one meetings.*

- *To do the work of a meeting organizer, you will assuredly get paid like a meeting organizer. To get paid like a keynote speaker, you need to become the keynote speaker.*

- *You need to choose some method to get yourself out of obscurity.*

REFLECTIONS

What is at least one benefit that you would experience if more people knew about you?

Would you currently put yourself in the category of being the meeting organizer or being the keynote speaker?

_____

What is a topic that you could speak on for forty-five minutes that would add value to your customers or referral partners?

_____

What platform most appeals to you at present (blog, vlog, podcast) and why?

_____

How frequently would you be able and willing to publish something on your preferred platform?

_____

9

THE CHARGE TO LEAD

You now understand new paradigms and strategies, encompassed within the Upstream Model, which allow you to extend your reach as a mentor and as a leader to get even more referrals from fewer relationships. These include simultaneously scaling your business and your identity, being the meeting keynote instead of the meeting organizer, and leveraging the power of video.

Even with all of that, if you do not understand and apply this last component, you may find short-term success. However, if you plan on having long-term, sustainable success, if you plan on creating significance, then you must understand this last vital factor. Your ability to not just show up as a mentor and leader but to become a leader will make all the difference.

FROM WORK TO WORKERS

"Justin, please don't bring your kids," a friend wrote in an email.

At the time, I spent most days of the week away from my family. I was often out of the house before they were up, and when I returned home in the evening, there was just time to help with mealtime and bedtime routines. Saturdays were a special day for us. So, amidst my offer to help a friend move residence on this day, a day that would already be a sacrifice, her request not to bring my kids did not sit well. Submitting to her appeal would not only be hard on my wife, leaving her with all six kids on a Saturday, but it would also be hard on me. I looked forward to this day of the week and the time that my kids and I could spend working and playing together. Additionally, I know that the way to help kids grow up to be good people is by giving them lots of opportunities to work and to serve other people. Helping my friend move was one of those opportunities that I did not want to miss.

So, despite her request, I politely and firmly pushed back and let her know that she was going to have to trust me on this one. If she wanted my help, my two oldest kids were a package deal.

As we wrapped up the move, you can imagine how good it felt to have my same friend pull me aside and tell me in a sincere tone, "Justin, your kids are so good and so helpful. I just want to keep them."

I will be the first to admit that I am fortunate to have great kids. Although they are not always *this* praise-worthy, when it mattered, they stepped up big. As she shared this genuine compliment, a feeling of pride and gratitude immediately came over me.

I then shared with her the following observation: "Isn't it interesting how just a generation or two ago people would purposely have more kids and large families because they needed additional help around their home or on their farm? More kids meant more capable workers. Now, just a generation or two later, people refrain from having large families and more kids because more kids do not mean more workers. More kids mean more work."

What changed?

It is almost as if parents from generations past knew that they could help develop their children from *being a burden* to instead being part of *lessening the burden*. They understood that they could grow their children into *becoming independent and helpful* rather than by allowing them to *remain dependents who always needed help.*

BECOMING A LEADER

As with the quest to help our children go from being "work for mom and dad" to "workers for mom and dad," the Upstream Model is about transforming you into something more valuable. You are required to become something more useful to your upstream partners, the referrals that they send, your family, your industry, your community, and the world at large.

The Upstream Model is not just a series of new tips, tricks, scripts, and tactics. With threats bearing down on your industry, surface-level help will not suffice. You need help to become something more a leader.

Additionally, this is not a method to just *guard* your commissions and margins or to *protect* you from industry disruption. Instead, the Upstream Model is a way for you to *earn and deserve your commissions* while helping you *rise above industry disruption*. As you execute the model correctly, both your upstream partners and their referrals will become some of your greatest defenders of keeping you well-compensated and at the center of the transaction. They recognize that it is in their best interests that you are. In short, the Upstream Model is an invitation for you to become a leader.

The world's foremost expert on the topic of leadership, John Maxwell, defined it this way: *"Leadership is influence. Nothing more, nothing less."*

You may have realized by now that the story of the Upstream Model is, in actuality, *my story*. It is my "hero's journey" as I have learned how to navigate to a place and become someone of more considerable influence. More importantly, though, it lays out a path for your journey from solicitor to vendor, from vendor to peer, and then on to mentor and leader. I am inviting you on this path because it is one that opens your possibilities to scalable income, quality of life, and impact.

In addition to the principles, strategies, and tactics shared thus far, to gain the full benefits of the Upstream Model, you must also embrace these fundamentals of becoming a leader.

Grow Yourself

When considering the most important attributes of a leader, often overlooked is the requirement that any great leader must first learn to be a good follower. No one becomes a great leader all on their own; they must follow and learn from others. The most impactful leaders in the world stand on the shoulders of giants and build from there.

I had the good fortune to interview bestselling author, social media celebrity, and world-renowned speaker and trainer Grant Cardone on my "Think Bigger Real Estate Show." The interview went like this:

> **Me**: So, Grant, tell us where you're at right now, which is going to inspire each and every one of us.
>
> **Grant**: Yes, so I'm at my church right now. I spent the last five days attending services here working on me and my blind spots. I'm here asking the questions "What don't I know?" and "What can I learn?"
>
> I've seen so many people reach high levels of success, particularly in the self-help and self-improvement space where guys are doing educational stuff. I mean, I'm literally thinking about their names in my mind right now, guys that are living that aren't living, if you know what I mean. I mean BIG giant individuals that have had tremendous success and legendary kinds of lifestyles. Some of these guys, most of these guys, quit learning. They quit being a student.
>
> So, anyway, I'm a student here. That's why I come here. I'm not leading. I'm not educating. I'm not doing a seminar. I'm just here to learn.

I agree with Grant. To be a great leader, you first have to be a great follower. You have to be deeply committed to the ongoing and never-ending pursuit of personal growth and development. Who you are and what you know today may be good enough to lead people today, but it will not be good enough to lead people tomorrow. Resting on your laurels of accomplishment, knowledge, or expertise will be a worse and worse idea as the world in which we live continues to thrive and change at an ever-accelerating pace.

Know Your People

To know someone is more than to know their contact information. It is not just having a robust database of likes and dislikes attached to the names therein. Tech already does that really well. Instead, it is having a human connection, one that is beyond the cerebral, extending to an emotional, even spiritual connection with people. This knowledge doesn't come through automation and drip campaigns. We experience and discover this more in-depth connection through genuine concern for and service toward other people.

I am often fascinated by the amount of time that service industry professionals spend on two things that seem to contradict one another:

1. Worrying about the rise of artificial intelligence and automation for fear of what parts of your job and income it will take away.

2. Committing too much of our efforts distancing ourselves from our customers by creating set-it and forget-it campaigns.

Well-known mortgage sales trainer and author of *High-Trust Selling,* Todd Duncan, was interviewing bestselling author Tim Sanders, who shared the following: *"The future is not about promotion. It's about an emotional connection. If you don't want competition, ask the questions they don't ask, say things they don't say, be in touch in unique ways, not superficial ways. The noise we send out as an industry does nothing for high trust."*

In this interview, Tim Sanders went on to share the following exchange that he had with a sales professional:

Tim: What's your biggest fear?

Sales Professional: That everything is going automated.

Tim: How do you communicate with your clients?

Sales Professional: We automate everything.

This scenario would be the equivalent of you being able to win a million dollars if you could beat Lebron James at either basketball or chess, and you choose basketball. While that might be fun, memorable, and create some great social media content, if everything depended on you beating Lebron, it would not be wise to challenge him to a one-on-one game of basketball. You may or may not be able to beat him at chess, but it at least becomes a winnable possibility.

Now, apply this metaphor to your business. If you want to win over the minds and hearts of upstream partners and the referrals that they send, competing against big tech firms at their own game by automating everything is not a winnable possibility.

My friend and local top local real estate agent Terry Sprague puts it this way: "*While others are doubling down on artificial intelligence, I'm doubling down on human intelligence.*"

Offering additional tactical advice, my friend and mentor Jay Marks says this: "*Stop chasing shiny objects* [latest tech] *and start chasing your past clients and your sphere of influence and service your clients as if you are their personal concierge. Then, tomorrow wake up and do it again.*"

Good leaders know their people, both their past and their present. Great leaders also come to know the intended future of their people.

By having the heart to do the work to uncover people's past and present, and desired future, you not only learn it for yourself, but you often help the person you lead to discover it for the first time themselves as well. Like two people working together on a beautiful painting, a powerful conversation between a leader and someone they serve about what that person's business or life could become is a powerful experience. A special bond and loyalty forms when you help someone to see a brighter, better, and clearer picture of their future than the one they were able to see before. You are changed, and so are they.

Love Your People

Several years ago, I paid $20,000 over two years to learn from a powerful educational organization and their bold leader. I credit him for changing the way that I see and interpret the marketplace, and for how to make uncommon and highly valued offers. Although the leader of the organization was, to this day, one of the smartest people that I have ever met, there were several instances in which, while sitting in his audience, he let us all know how he really felt about us.

I remember one instance when somebody from the audience raised their hand to ask what I thought was a fair question. This leader bolted from the back of the room in a fit of rage and yelled the following expletive-filled diatribe: *"Do you see those cameras? Do you know why those cameras are there? It's to record this material so that I don't have to be in these rooms putting up with this bullshit!"*

I decided at that moment that this guy wasn't going to get any more of my money. Although many offers were made for me to continue with the organization, gaining access to the compelling content that his courses offered, I declined. I later determined that for me to follow someone, I needed to know that I was more than just a pawn in their game. I needed to know that they genuinely wanted me to have a better business and a better life, regardless of what I could do for them.

As I reflect on leaders in my life, there have been others that I knew had genuine love and concern for me and whomever they served. One such was my second high-school football coach, Coach Crace, to whom I introduced you previously. Many community members and high school football fans marveled about how Coach was able to take a program from startup mode to winning a state championship in such a short time. While they were fortunate to have some tremendous and smart athletes go through the school system at that time, so did a lot of other schools. To me, the difference was that we, as players, knew that Coach Crace loved us. We knew what he sacrificed for us and appreciated the time he spent laughing with us, crying with us, working out with us, and on and on. As a result of his influence, we were willing to listen to him, be pushed by him, and be rallied by him. Ultimately, we were willing to give our all for him and our common cause, day in and day out. He got the very best out of us, which, I believe, was the difference.

We've all heard it said that people don't care how much you know until they know how much you care. I believe that to be true. One way to test this is to go on to social media and share some of your most profound insights and see what kind of interaction you get. Then, find people you know and comment on some of what is happening in their life. Now, compare the interaction.

If your experience is like mine, you'll find that you are much more empowered to influence and lead people by taking an interest in what is going on in their life than by trying to get them interested in you.

World-renowned author, speaker, and trainer Dale Carnegie, in his classic book *How to Win Friends and Influence People*, taught this same principle this way: *"You will accomplish more by developing a sincere interest in people than you ever will by trying to get people interested in you."*

When our upstream partners and their referrals know that we genuinely care for them and that they are more than just pawns in our game, they will find themselves willing and wanting to be led by us.

Serve Your People

When I accepted the position to work as a title and escrow sales executive, I interviewed with and went to work for a man by the name of Bill Thomas. Bill was one of those leaders that you just didn't want to disappoint. I was not intimidated by Bill, but I respected Bill. Why is it that Bill commanded so much respect?

At first, when I would introduce Bill to others in my industry, I would say, "This is Bill Thomas. Bill runs our operation, and so I get to work for Bill."

Immediately, Bill would always correct me in a genuine and humble tone by saying, "Actually, we both work for Old Republic Title, and Justin and I work together."

When first going to work for Bill, I heard the story of how serious a responsibility he took hiring someone new. Rather than just seeing a "new hire," Bill would see in his mind plates at their dinner table. He knew that by hiring this person, he was committing to do everything within his power to lead the organization in such a way that would ensure there was food on those plates at that dinner table.

Both of these are seemingly small things, but they tell a story of how Bill saw leadership. His job (and he reiterated this often) was to work for those he served that he might remove obstacles for them that they might be able to do their best work. These comments were not just lip service. We saw and felt his sacrifice and saw his service on our behalf each and every day.

Bestselling author, speaker, and trainer Simon Sinek says, **"Leadership is not about being in charge. Leadership is about taking care of those in your charge."**

Part of serving people is removing ego from the equation. I've been in roles and organizations where I have felt that the leader wanted me to succeed so long as my success did not eclipse his or her accomplishments. My potential with the organization, or my ceiling, became controlled by the leader above me. Their willingness to promote my growth and success was contingent upon not surpassing their growth and success.

At other times I've been in roles where I knew that my leader's success came in part from the success that I had. There was no ceiling from them but rather nothing but empowerment to recognize and pursue my ambition and potential. Gandhi put it this way: *"A sign of a good leader is not how many followers you have but how many leaders you create."*

Similarly, John Maxwell, in *Five Levels of Leadership*, describes Level Four as the People Development Level, or the Reproduction Level. Here, your leadership reproduces new leaders. Leaders who best serve are leaders who help to create and produce more leaders. It's hard to fathom the endless ripple effect that this would have if all leaders had Level Four be the floor of their leadership. You can imagine the success that you can create together with your upstream partners when they know that you are offering help to them because of your genuine love and concern for them.

DON'T GIVE THE SERMON, BE THE SERMON

While participating in different service and leadership roles in my job, my business, my church, my community, and of course, my home, I often have to remind myself that more is caught than taught. It doesn't matter how much I teach and preach to others around me; they pay more attention to the sermon that I'm *living* than the one that I'm *speaking*. The same is true for you.

Referencing Maxwell, his fifth level of leadership, the highest level, is when people follow you because of what you represent. When someone chooses to go with you as a product or service provider, it is typically because of at least two reasons:

1. The direct value that your product or service offers to them. For example, I am using an Apple computer because I love the functionality of Apple products.

2. The indirect value that someone gets by having their brand affiliated with your brand. Continuing my example, I became interested in using an Apple computer, and continue using it today, in part because other creators and leaders also use Apple products. By working from an Apple computer, it tells me and others that I am like those other creators and leaders. Apple's brand and story help to accurately reinforce my brand and to tell my story.

As superficial as this may sound, I guarantee that, at least to some degree, you follow similar patterns.

Just as companies and products have brands, so do we as individuals, and so do we as leaders. When we live what we teach, our life becomes a consistent story and a consistent brand. This consistency allows others to be clear on who we are, what we stand for, and the mission and purpose with which we engage. They can more easily determine if we are in alignment with them. Those we lead or aspire to lead can decide if aligning their brand with ours, through following us, learning from us, and partnering with us, is consistent with their brand and helpful in telling their own story and fulfilling their mission.

We Need You to Lead

Studies from brain scientists show how our society today, as a result of a lack of leadership in the home, has created a larger group of people than ever before that are lacking emotional maturity and the ability to lead others. Our society is in a desperate shortage of leaders at home, in business, in industry, and in communities.

In your industry, with the rise of technology designed to replace what you do, and get paid, for a living, the only way forward for you to remain well-paid and in the transaction is to lead and to become a better and stronger leader. By growing yourself, by knowing your people, by loving your people, and by living by example, you are accepting the charge to lead. You will be thinking bigger, waking up to the potential that is within you, living in pursuit of that potential so that you can live, give, and serve abundantly. To inspire and help that to happen for you is the mission I am on.

ASSERTIONS

- *The Upstream Model is an invitation to become something more, to become a leader.*
- *Good leaders grow themselves.*
- *Good leaders know their people and love their people.*
- *Good leaders live the sermon.*

REFLECTIONS

On a scale of 1 to 5, where would you put your current ability to influence and lead people in your home?

_____

On a scale of 1 to 5, where would you put your current ability to influence and lead people in your job or business?

_____

On a scale of 1 to 5, where would you put your current ability to influence and lead your upstream partners?

_____

From what you learned about leadership from this chapter, what can you do to become a better leader in your business and in your community?

_____

10

TIME FOR BIGGER THINKING

While massive tech companies continue spending billions of dollars attempting to minimize and replace what common professionals do and get paid, you can rest assured that you are no longer common. The Upstream Model has given you a framework to grow your business and to grow yourself. The value that you bring to your upstream partners and their referrals is now out of reach from your competitors, including big tech.

Now you know how to get more referrals from fewer relationships. Specifically, you know how to go from courting hundreds of people in your database to receive just a few client referrals to, instead, courting a few vital upstream partners in your database to receive hundreds of client referrals.

Now you know how to go from being a common solicitor and vendor to being an uncommon peer.

Now you know how to go from being just a peer to being a mentor and a leader.

Now you know how to follow the pattern of the most valuable companies in the world by thinking and acting like a technology platform company.

Now you know how to extend your reach, simultaneously scaling both your identity and your business.

Now you know, at a time when there is a massive leadership shortage, how to become a stronger leader and how to step up and lead.

Now the only thing that can stop you from living, giving, and serving abundantly is if you allow those six inches between your ears get in your way. So, let's address that now.

My mission and my passion are to help you to "Think Bigger"—to wake you up to the potential that is within you and then to inspire and help you to live your life in pursuit of that potential, so that you can live, give, and serve abundantly. That is one of my life's primary purposes. As you commit to following me, learning with me, and taking action, I commit to doing everything within my power to help make this a reality for you.

Stephen R. Covey taught that *"things are created spiritually before they are created physically."*

In other words, you create things in your mind before you create them in your life. Before you take new action, like taking the first step in implementing the Upstream Model, your brain takes you through a split-second evaluation process. An oversimplified explanation goes something like this:

NEW ACTION CONSIDERED > ANTICIPATED GOOD OUTCOME > YOU TAKE ACTION

NEW ACTION CONSIDERED > ANTICIPATED BAD or NO OUTCOME > YOU DON'T TAKE ACTION

To begin the process of changing your businesses and your life for the better, opening yourself up to increased possibilities, you must recognize the flaw in the above internal evaluation process that causes you to take action or not. How you determine whether you are going to have either an "anticipated good outcome" or an "anticipated bad/no outcome" is often not grounded in facts or real data. Instead, your projected outcome is often illogical, emotional, and flawed.

The remarkable thing is that it only takes one thought to change everything. That thought can be as simple as, *I want this to work for me.* This one hopeful thought is like a seed that, when nurtured, can grow into the confident belief that *"this will work for me."* And with this belief, you will be encouraged to take the first step. From that will come results, which will give you the knowledge that *"this is working for me!"*

The million-dollar question then becomes *How do I nurture the hope within that me that "I want this to work for me" enough to where it turns into the belief that "this will work for me"?*

The answer is simple. If you don't yet have that belief, you can borrow it from someone else who does. You can borrow it from me. Allow the data and facts from my journey, together with those gathered from interviewing, consulting, and coaching hundreds and hundreds of additional professionals, to give you the belief that this *will* work for you so that you take your first step.

The first step in making this work for you is to accept my offer to help make this model work for you in the most significant way possible. You can find my mentorship and leadership at *upstreammodel.com*.

My final request of everyone reading this, which is the same way that I close out each episode of the "Think Bigger Real Estate Show," is an invitation and a charge. It consists of three simple words:

GO THINK BIGGER!!!

Made in the USA
Monee, IL
25 April 2022